Praise for Caitlin Flanagan's
Girl Land

"Flanagan's examination of the lives of teenage girls will resonate.... I snapped up this book with a burning hunger.... Read *Girl Land* to reminisce about your own dates, proms, periods, and panics."　　　　—Susan Ager, *Minneapolis Star Tribune*

"Flanagan is not antifeminist, or controversial. In fact, her methods and attitudes come straight out of the women's studies classes I took at college in the late '70s, and her outrage on behalf of girls coming of age in the 'Brush Your Teeth with a Bottle of Jack' era will feel just right to most women in our age group.... These right-wing-sounding views will likely get no argument from most liberal moms.... Flanagan's not a hypocrite."　　　　—Marion Winik, *Newsday*

"Witty, wry, and breezily entertaining.... It's a topic rife for analysis—about those angsty and confusing years between girlhood and womanhood, and the milestones (both physical and emotional) young women must overcome to reach the other side. It's got a catchy title, and a compelling cover....The book is a trip down memory lane, well-researched social history....A compelling history of dating....The writing flows easily, and Flanagan's personal stories are peppered throughout....Extreme? Sure. But that's the Flanagan we know and love."

　　　　—Jessica Bennett, *Daily Beast*

"Flanagan's most concentrated historical effort occurs in the chapter about dating, which is the book's best. She pulls telling quotes from novels aimed at adolescent girls and presents us with delightful primary sources....She also culls decades' worth of dating guidebooks, parsing them for now-obsolete conventions, and concluding that most perform the rhetorical feat of disguising 'quiet safety mechanisms' as points of etiquette." —Alice Gregory, *Boston Globe*

"*Girl Land* aims to provide a historically based account of 'the traditional milestones' that mark the American girl's entrée into the adult world. There are some interesting bits on pre–*Our Bodies, Ourselves* advice manuals for girls and on pre-*Carrie* proms."—Polly Rosenwaike, *San Francisco Chronicle*

"The conservative social critic Caitlin Flanagan identifies a stretch between girlhood and womanhood as a developmental chrysalis." —Lisa Schwarzbaum, *Entertainment Weekly*

"Flanagan may be more sophisticated than many conservative ideologues." —Katie Roiphe, *Slate*

"Part social critique, part memoir, and, like Flanagan, a little contrarian, *Girl Land* is both a moving account of what it means for girls to leave childhood behind, and a chiding of society for not providing a more positive environment through which to make the transition." —Chelsea Allison, *Vogue*

"A compelling, convincing case for more parental involvement in girls' lives." —*Kirkus Reviews*

"Flanagan offers observations and takes a more sustained look at girls as they leave childhood and head into the treacherous passage of adolescence.... She has been the middle-class mom's Alpha Girl, the clever queen of the devastating put-down.... In *Girl Land* her tone has lost none of its edge.... Smart and occasionally maddening."
—Emma Gilbey Keller, *New York Times Book Review*

"Flanagan is roundly brilliant but also incredibly tough."
—Alexander Nazaryan, *New York Daily News*

"If you were ever a teenage girl, and especially if you are the parent of one now, you will likely be lured to Caitlin Flanagan's *Girl Land* the way a thirteen-year-old is enticed toward *Twilight*.... Informative.... Flanagan's desire to protect girls is admirable." —Jennifer Miller, *Christian Science Monitor*

"A collection of boldly prescriptive, occasionally autobiographical essays.... Provocateur Caitlin Flanagan paints a picture of teen girlhood in which men and boys can be dangerous.... Whether or not you agree, you'll be absorbed by her commentary on the glamorous marketing of sanitary products and the now-slippery definition of virginity."
—Lori Gottlieb, *More*

"In exploring rites of passage like proms and first loves, as well as rituals like diary-keeping, this new book by Caitlin Flanagan shows how the concept of girlhood has changed over time, from the roaring '20s to the buttoned-up '50s to today's e-culture. While the book does have a parenting component, moms and non-moms alike will be intrigued by Flanagan's reflections on the significant impact teenage milestones have on girls' future adult lives."   —*Glo*

"Flanagan is never afraid to take a sharpened stick to the hornets' nest.... Flanagan's central premise is not only worthwhile, it's exactly the sort of argument that so few in media dare to make, butting up against both liberal notions about freedom of speech and pornography and the free-to-be-you-and-me universe that most middle-class feminists of a certain age grew up in.... Flanagan weaves quite a compelling tale."
—Heather Havrilesky, *BookForum*

"In *Girl Land,* Flanagan has shifted her focus from the women running the home to the girls growing up in it.... The subject is rich material—the awkwardness of coming of age sexually and emotionally while still living under your parents' roof. At least since the sexual revolution, teenage girls have lived a kind of double life—simultaneously children and adults, they're stranded in an odd half-in, half-out period of extended girlhood that confuses everyone involved."
—Meghan O'Rourke, *New York*

"Flanagan's new book, *Girl Land,* is another plea for a return to traditional roles, to a simpler time, when girls were weaned on romantic fantasies rather than sexts and porn sites.... Like many of us, Caitlin Flanagan has a problem with our 'crass, corrosive, sexualized' culture. She wants more control over what girls are exposed to, and urges parents to stay involved in their daughters' lives. I'm on board with all of this."
— Rebecca Odes, *Babble*

"It's Flanagan's fearlessness and unexpected (if frequently misguided) compassion for women that makes her a literary hero of mine.... Her new book, *Girl Land,* is full of sympathy for girls and women. Page after page is devoted to outlining the many ways in which girls are particularly vulnerable to physical and sexual violence and emotional harm.... Her earnest desire to protect girls' emotional well-being and bodily integrity belies her hostility toward the women's movement; in truth, she's a good deal more sympathetic to the ideals of feminism than many contemporary writers.... It's hard not to admire her nerve.... Flanagan is smart, candid, and confident to a fault.... She's sharp, authoritative, and gleefully, unapologetically mean.... The firmer one's convictions and the stronger one's sense of self, the easier it is to read (and enjoy!) writers like Flanagan and the late, great Christopher Hitchens.... Caitlin Flanagan does not care if people think she's mean. What could be more feminist than that?"
— Raina Lipsitz, *The Atlantic*

"I like that she insists on the value of a safe, steady domestic sphere, of staying home with children, of two-parent families, of the pulled-tight parental involvement that ensures teenagers have some time and space to themselves."

—Kate Carraway, *National Post*

"An alarming treatise on the perils of postmodern girl-hood.... It's tough to imagine how any halfway-conscious parent can argue with Flanagan's assertion that our hyper-sexualized culture poses particular risks for girls. For those still unconvinced, there are reams of reports from groups like the American Psychological Association describing links between the rising sexualization of girls and their struggles with depression, eating disorders, promiscuity, and poor self-image.... *Girl Land* accurately captures the emotional truth behind these studies.... Happily, parents still can use books like Flanagan's and studies like those circulated by the APA as helpful reminders that when it comes to raising girls today, the challenges are real and the stakes are high."

—Colleen Carroll Campbell, *St. Louis Post-Dispatch*

"Flanagan is a wickedly sharp stylist capable of surprising in-sights.... Has anyone ever described the bewilderment of menarche so well? Remarking that 'getting your period' makes it sound like an acquisition along the lines of 'getting your own Princess telephone,' Flanagan again demonstrates her knack for the perfect detail.... She describes [her own girlhood] with great clarity and expressiveness." —Ruth Franklin, *The Daily*

"Flanagan's writing is alluring and memorable....She does not equivocate, and her style gives her an aesthetic leg up on some of her more mealy-penned critics. I admire her chops....An interesting, discursive, and occasionally compelling account of the evolution of the American teenage girl....It seems like Flanagan has written two books—one book is a quiet look at her own young womanhood, set against a brief history of the rearing of young women. I found her sympathetic portrait of Patty Hearst moving, and I love that Flanagan, she of the Dior bedspreads, talks blood puddles and clots as she describes the carnage of menarche.... *Girl Land* is a working-out of something deep and personal, offering parental guidance."   —Lydia Kiesling, *The Millions*

Also by Caitlin Flanagan

To Hell with All That: Loving and Loathing Our Inner Housewife

Girl Land

Caitlin Flanagan

A REAGAN ARTHUR BOOK

BACK BAY BOOKS

LITTLE, BROWN AND COMPANY

NEW YORK   BOSTON   LONDON

Reagan Arthur / Back Bay Books
Little, Brown and Company
Hachette Book Group
237 Park Avenue, New York, NY 10017
reaganarthurbooks.com

Originally published in hardcover by Reagan Arthur Books / Little, Brown and
Company, January 2012
First Reagan Arthur / Back Bay Books paperback edition, February 2013

Reagan Arthur Books is an imprint of Little, Brown and Company, a division of
Hachette Book Group. The Reagan Arthur Books name and logo are trademarks of
Hachette Book Group, Inc.

The publisher is not responsible for websites (or their content) that are not owned by
the publisher.

The Hachette Speakers Bureau provides a wide range of authors for speaking events.
To find out more, go to hachettespeakersbureau.com or call (866) 376-6591.

Portions of this book have appeared in *The Atlantic* in slightly different form. The
author is grateful to the Hearst Corporation for permission to reprint material from
Seventeen.

Library of Congress Cataloging-in-Publication Data
Flanagan, Caitlin.
  Girl land / Caitlin Flanagan. — 1st ed.
      p. cm.
  "A Reagan Arthur Book."
  Includes bibliographical references.
  ISBN 978-0-316-06598-6 (hc) / 978-0-316-06599-3 (pb)
  1. Teenage girls — United States. 2. Teenage girls — Psychology. 3. Adolescence. I.
Title.
  HQ798.F58 2012
  305.235'20973 — dc23   2011024934

10 9 8 7 6 5 4 3 2 1

RRD-C

Printed in the United States of America

For Rob, as always
And for Conor and Patrick

Spring and Fall
To a young child

Margaret, are you grieving
Over Goldengrove unleaving?
Leaves, like the things of man, you
With your fresh thoughts care for, can you?
Ah! as the heart grows older
It will come to such sights colder
By and by, nor spare a sigh
Though worlds of wanwood leafmeal lie;
And yet you will weep and know why.
Now no matter, child, the name:
Sorrow's springs are the same.
Nor mouth had, no nor mind, expressed
What heart heard of, ghost guessed:
It is the blight man was born for,
It is Margaret you mourn for.

Gerard Manley Hopkins, 1880

Contents

Girl Land

CHAPTER ONE

Girl Land

Every woman I've known describes her adolescence as the most psychologically intense period of her life. Her memories of it are vivid: the exquisite friendships and first loves, the ways in which the products of popular culture—the movies and television shows and music—of the day didn't just inform her emotional life but became a part of it. She remembers, too, the particular and bittersweet tenor of the time, the way her teenage years, for which she spent so much of her early life preparing and practicing, constituted an end to her childhood. Emerging into sexual maturity comes with very different realities and vulnerabilities for girls than it does for boys, and the process of entering it is thus more psychologically and emotionally intense. This is Girl Land: the attenuated leave-taking, the gathering awareness of what is being lost forever. Becoming a woman is an act partly of nature and partly of self-invention; Girl Land is the place and time in which all of this is worked out.

The work of Girl Land is eternal and unchanging. We see its signposts across time and cultures: a girl's sudden need to withdraw from the world for a while and to inhabit a secret emotional life, is as true of the nineteenth-century British schoolgirl as it is of the American teenager of today. She slips into that private place during her sulks and silences, during her endless hours alone in her room, or even just when she's gazing out the classroom window while all of modern European history, or the niceties of the *passé composé,* sluice past her. She is a creature designed for a richly lived interior life (and for all the things that come with such a life: reading, writing in a diary, listening to music while she stares out the window and dreams) in a way most boys are not. Her most elemental psychological needs— to be undisturbed while she works out the big questions, to be hidden from view while still in plain sight, to have deeply, sometimes unbearably empathic responses to the sorrows and excitements of others—are met precisely through this act of drawing within herself, of disappearing for a while. What is she doing? She's coming to terms with her emergence as a sexual creature, with everything good and everything frightening that accompanies this transformation. She is also mourning the loss of her little girlhood, in a way that boys typically don't mourn the loss of their childhoods.

One of the signal differences between adolescent girls and boys is that a boy does not fetishize the tokens of his childhood. An eighth-grade boy doesn't catch sight of his old Legos and feel a sudden surge of heartbreak; he either walks right past them or sits down and tinkers with them until something else comes along to distract him. They are not the marker of something lost to him forever. But how many fully liberated young college women will bring something from the lost continent of little girlhood to their new lives—the worn teddy bear that sits, half ironically, on the dorm room dresser; the glass animal bought on the long-ago holiday. These are objects she regards with mixed emotions, emotions that few young men can begin to understand.

The emotional life of a little girl is drenched with romance. Modern mothers, planning to raise independent, strong-minded daughters, are very often confronted with a pre-school girl's stubborn attraction to princess costumes and stories and toys. A girl entering adolescence is making the discovery that female sexuality—a force more complex than she has ever imagined—is intimately enmeshed with romance. A girl at this stage of her life realizes that dreams of being in love, of having a boyfriend, a husband, a family of her own, depend upon sex. The awareness begins with menstruation, something she may have been waiting for eagerly but that brings with it certain raw truths: that emerging female sexuality is intrinsically bound in the blood and profundity that are the truth of human reproduction. The toll and consequence of sexuality fall much more harshly on women than on men, and as a girl enters adolescence this becomes starkly true to her. Furthermore, she learns that with the advent of sexual maturity, she is becoming attractive not just to the boys her age, but also to grown men, some of whom do not mean her well. Sexual danger enters her life, and even the ways in which she is taught to protect herself from it serve to highlight its reality. She longs to be in two places at once: the safety of little girlhood, with the stuffed animals and the jump ropes and the simplicity of childhood, but also in the new place, in the arms of a lover whom she wants to ravish her, to deliver her to new shores. Figuring all of this out is why girls want to spend so much time alone in their bedrooms with the doors closed. One of the biggest problems for parents of these teenagers is that they never know who is going to come barreling out of that sacred space: the adorable little girl who wants to cuddle, or the hard-eyed young woman who has left it all behind.

We sense that, despite all of our efforts to change and demystify and improve the experience of female puberty, it has somehow become even more difficult than it ever was. There is a paradox at the heart of contemporary Girl Land, and this paradox makes the emotional experience of female adolescence more intense and difficult than ever. On the one hand, never in history have girls had so many opportunities, or shared so fully in the kind of power that was only recently reserved for boys. Girls now outperform boys on the SAT; women outnumber men in college, and we are nearing a point at which women will outnumber men in the country's law and medical schools. In the space of a few short decades, the entire landscape of what is possible for a girl has changed dramatically. But on the other hand, at the exact same moment, we have seen the birth of a common culture that is openly contemptuous of girls and young women. At every turn, girls—even the most carefully raised and deeply loved—are surrounded by a popular culture that exhorts them to think of themselves as sexually disposable creatures. The frank message of a thousand songs and websites and comic rants is that women exist merely to please men. Some of the best and brightest girls have come to believe this poisonous message; we need look no further than their millions of Facebook pages to see that this is true.

The current culture, with its driving imperatives of exhibitionism, of presenting oneself to the world in the most forward and blasting way possible, has made the experience of Girl Land especially charged and difficult. The sexually explicit music, the endless hard-core and even fetish pornography available twenty-four hours a day on the Internet, the crudeness of so much of the national conversation and the ways that technology has made it so that there is almost no such thing as a private experience anymore—all of this is hard on everyone, but I would contend that it is most punishing to girls. This is a terrible moment in which to be a thoughtful person or an introspective one, and so it is a terrible one in which to be a citizen of Girl Land. Never in American history have we seen a period in which the romantic impulse and the lyrical sensibility have been driven so completely to ground. And these are two forms of expression that have always been vital to the girl heart. Once, men were a significant part of creating that lyricism, because it was the key to the lock; to get the girl was to woo the girl—and in that process, however unintentionally, the man came to know the girl herself. Grandmother may have been shocked by "Lay, Lady, Lay"—"Whatever colors you have in your mind/I'll show them to you and you'll see them shine"—but there is no denying that the song's appeal was not just erotic, but also deeply romantic. Compare it to the most popular love song of the summer of 2010 as I write, a Rihanna-Eminem duet called "Love the Way You Lie," in which an abusive boyfriend, desperate to do anything to earn back his girlfriend's trust, makes the soul-wrenching commitment of a lifetime: "Next time I'm pissed/I'll aim my fist at the dry wall." A promise to build a life on. Still, though, one with a caveat: if she ever tries to leave him again, "I'ma tie her to the bed and set the house on fire."

In this book, I've set out to examine the traditional milestones of American Girl Land, the events or experiences that mark the passage out of childhood and into womanhood. I wanted to see in what ways they have changed, and in what ways their essential meanings have remained the same. Some of these milestone events are physical ones, such as menstruation and sexual initiation. Others are culturally constructed, such as proms and diary-keeping. What is it like for a girl to get her first period, now that the event is no longer a harbinger of a process—reproduction—that might be gravely dangerous to her? Why do proms still mean so much to American girls, now that conventional dating—of the type that the formal dance was meant to be the apogee—has now all but died out? All of these passages are still understood to be significant in the lives of girls, but for what reasons? This book examines the great and unchanging questions of Girl Land, as they are asked and answered in the ever-shifting landscape of today's youth culture.

CHAPTER TWO

Dating

OF ALL THE CHANGES THAT have taken place in Girl Land since the advent of modernity, none has been more radical than dating. The death of the old courtship system, in which middle-class parents were deeply involved in their daughters' romantic lives, which unfolded largely in their own homes, under near-constant supervision, was a revolutionary development. This change, from the old system of a boy "calling" on a girl, in the company of her parents, to one in which he took her out on a date without supervision, was unprecedented, and altered the landscape of Girl Land forever. It gave middle-class girls a kind of power they had never before had, but it also exposed them to dangers they had never before encountered.

The essential and inescapable paradox of dating is that while girls have just as much of an interest in it as boys— in fact, as we shall see, to a certain extent, girls invented the custom—they have far more at risk in going out alone with a member of the opposite sex. Much of the cultural conversation involving girls and dating has been a process of informing them about these dangers. The terms of the conversation were at first highly coded and filled with euphemism (about what to do if a boy got "fresh," about the importance of bringing "mad money" on a date), then increasingly frank and frightening (with descriptions of "date rape" and "teen dating violence"). Because Girl Land is drenched in romance—as well as in developing eros—the idea of being out with a boy is exciting, dreamy. But teens of the opposite sex enter those situations on unequal footing: if someone is to be forced into sexual situations, or beaten up, or left with the consequences of pregnancy, if someone is to get the worst of a variety of terrible things that can happen in the privacy and seclusion of a date, it's going to be the girl.

Moreover, girls are notorious for being unimpressed by the kind of boys who seem safe and mild-mannered. When I was a girl, one of the most popular board games was Milton Bradley's Mystery Date, in which players tried to collect the right outfits and accessories to go out on whichever date turned out to be waiting for her behind the white plastic door in the middle of the board. There was the Beach Date and the Formal Dance Date and the Bowling Date and the Picnic Date—each of them handsome boys, each capable of whisking you off to a day of unfettered excitement, but if you didn't have the bathing suit and towel or the proper dress and high heels, you were getting left at home. There was an even worse fate that could befall you on Mystery Date: you could open the door and find none of the dreamy daters, but instead the "dud," who was a grease monkey with a five o'clock shadow dressed in a mechanic's uniform. Everything about the paradoxes and vulnerabilities of midcentury dating was conveyed in this character: he wasn't a nerd or a geek, he was clearly someone who had dropped out of school altogether and who had so little respect for the girl that he hadn't even washed up. He wasn't just a dud, he was also vaguely threatening. As if that weren't bad enough, the dud could ruin you: just opening the door to him meant you lost all of your accumulated outfits and accessories, the Milton Bradley equivalent of getting into trouble and being kicked out of your good home. But here's what the game makers and the parents of girls didn't predict: Girls liked the dud. They *really* liked him. They thought he was sexy and cool and kind of...dangerous. All over the Internet you can find women my age admitting that they secretly hoped they would get the dud, who was also sometimes called the "bum."

The exact nature of what does and doesn't constitute a date has changed over the years. In the fifties it might have been a relatively formal event in which a boy drove to a girl's home and picked her up for an evening out, and today it might consist of them hooking up at an unchaperoned party. But the term has stayed with us, and the subject is of great and enduring interest to girls. Magazines for girls still carry starry-eyed articles about dating. When social workers in the early 2000s discovered an increase in the incidence of boys who beat up their girlfriends, they called the new phenomenon "teen dating violence," because "dating," as a term of art, still means something specific to young people. Whether it was the mad money handed out by fathers, or the instructions revealed in old guidebooks about what to do if a boy got fresh with you on a date, or the well-meaning counsel on the existence and prevention of date rape, the net result is the same for girls. They learn that underneath the glittering surface of dating lies the possibility of danger. And part of the allure of dating is that very danger—as the fondess for the Milton Bradley dud and songs like "Love the Way You Lie" can make clear.

A month before my senior year of high school, my parents and I moved from Berkeley, where I had grown up, to Long Island, where I was enrolled in a public high school in a bedroom community, and I attempted to survive long enough to get into college and escape. Emotionally troubled and desperately homesick, I decided that the thing to do was to find a good boyfriend, whose female friends would become my friends, and whose social world would become my own. That's what girls did in those days, in high school: we had boyfriends. We didn't call it "going steady";

that was a fifties term. We called it "going with" somebody, but it meant the same thing. I set my sights on a particular boy who was a varsity athlete on a top team. He was strong and powerful-looking and he didn't say much, so I was free to project any personality I chose onto his blank canvas. Sold.

One day in late November he offered to drive me home from school, which seemed like an excellent, even propitious turn of events. My parents were away that day, meeting with my father's publisher in the city. I could invite him inside without having to worry about them hovering; we could hang out. In the preceding eight weeks, absent any actual conversation, I had assigned him certain habits of mind and qualities of character; we were the Titania and Bottom of our high school. At last, with this ride, our destiny—as a love match in the making and as a union that would solve several of my most pressing problems—was at hand. But right away, things got off on the wrong foot. In the car, he seemed quieter than I had imagined him to be; I peppered him with flattering questions, but he said almost nothing. We got to my house, and I took him on a little tour. For reasons having to do with the difference in real estate values in the San Francisco Bay Area and Long Island, it was quite a place, and he seemed impressed by it—almost cowed by it—in a way that embarrassed me a bit. But there was something more to his reaction to the house, although I don't know if I realized this at that moment or if it emerged during the endless, self-recriminating hours I later devoted to reliving and reexamining the events of that afternoon: I think the house surprised him. My arrival at the last possible moment at school had suggested perhaps that I was a marginal person, part of some vague train of family miseries and lost chances. That I didn't come from much and could be treated accordingly. The house had a pond at the bottom of a garden, and he stood for a moment looking out the dining room window toward it, and then—suddenly, impulsively—he suggested that we go to the beach. I remember trying to convince him that we should stay in the house—I could make us a snack, we could watch some television—but he was adamant; it was the most animated he'd been the whole time, and so I agreed. And that was my mistake.

We had hardly left my driveway when I realized I didn't like this boy. He had gone from being quiet to being almost mute. Why didn't I tell him to just take me back home? Politeness, mostly, and also the gathering momentum of the afternoon, of having agreed to go. It seemed I'd just have to see the thing through.

At the beach, there was no parking attendant and no lifeguard; the snack kiosks were boarded up. There was no one in sight. I hadn't expected it to be deserted. I was from California; I knew kids who surfed year-round. Almost as soon as he parked, the boy leaned over and kissed me. If I live a hundred years, I'll never forget the shock of that kiss; it was aggressive and artless, and completely unconnected—obviously—to any feelings for me at all. He just sort of lunged over and landed it on me, and I reacted to it by reaching up my hand and pushing him away. I remember all of these moments very clearly: the way I pushed him away from me, confident that he would stop what he was doing when he realized I didn't like it. I was sixteen; I'd been in situations like this before; I knew what to do. But then he did something that no one had ever done to me before: he ignored my protests. He kept going, pushing himself all the way against me and then reaching for the zipper of my coat. I struggled away, started to say something, but he was on me again, and I had a vague thought: he's not getting the message. It seemed important to find some other way to let him know I wasn't up for anything he had in mind; he was apparently an obtuse kid. I moved away, he didn't stop, and that's when I realized the truth of the situation: I was the one who wasn't getting the message.

It was a few years before the term date rape would enter the national consciousness. It's hard to explain how deeply that concept would change the way all of us felt about the time we spent alone with boys and young men, the rights we had, and the ones the men did not. When I first saw the term, part of an information sheet posted in the lounge of a women's bathroom in my college, I stared at it for half an hour. You could be on a date, something you had agreed on freely, a set of risks you had freely agreed to accept, but if a boy forced himself on you, you could still be the victim of a rape? We just didn't know that then. We sort of thought that if things got out of hand, then it was our fault. As it turned out, there was a long cultural tradition dedicated to making us believe it, but at the time I was at the beach with that boy, all I knew was that something terrible was happening and that it was somehow my fault. I wasn't nice enough or pretty enough or entertaining enough to be worth decent treatment.

When that boy tried to force me to have sex with him, I reacted with something more than fear, more than anger, more than panic. I was suffused with a single, blinding emotion: outrage. I yelled at him, I kicked him, and I went for the door handle. He stopped. This was a kid who was applying—and would get accepted—to the best schools, and to this day I wonder if that's what saved me. I created a context in which, if he had pressed ahead, there would be no way to interpret his actions other than as an assault. In short order, we were driving back to my house in silence. He let me out of the car and drove away.

Now, after so many years, this story doesn't seem like much: a sixteen-year-old girl who went out with a boy she didn't know well and who turned out to be a boor but not a monster. He did stop, after all. But I can't tell you how much the experience shamed and scared me, how much I felt it had been a reflection on me and on my shortcomings. Deeply woven into my sense of the experience were the lessons I had learned from an informal but relentless curriculum, one delivered by the girl culture I was growing up in—teen magazines, romantic novels and movies and television shows I loved, as well as comments from adults and older girls. Embedded in all of that, never directly stated but nonetheless very clear, were the twin notions that it was a girl's responsibility not to allow a date to get "out of hand" if she didn't want it to and also that only a boy who didn't respect you would attempt to force you to do something against your will. "Respect" was the word that was always used in this context, although it seems to me now only to underscore the inequality of power that exists on a date: my safety was not grounded in my own ability to defend myself, only in my hope that he would choose to respect what I wanted.

But here's the bigger question: why in the world would I, a slight sixteen-year-old girl, have ever thought it was a sensible and safe thing to go first to an empty house and then to a deserted beach with a boy I hardly knew, whom my parents had never met, about whom I knew almost nothing at all? I was not a particularly levelheaded kid, but in making that decision, I was in no way violating any norms of proper behavior for a relatively cosseted and well-loved middle-class daughter. In fact, if my mother had happened to call the house that afternoon, and I had told her I was on the way to Cedar Beach with a boy from my school, she would have said good for you. I'd felt safe because I lived during a historical moment when dating—the catchall term for any event whereby two romantically inclined young people go on an excursion without any chaperone—was over a half-century old. Dating, filled with the excitement of romance and young sexuality, but also laden with dark, indirect warnings about a world of dangers and snares, had for so long been the prerogative of

Girl Land, one of the main points of leaving little girlhood behind, that I was behaving according to every television show and teen guidebook and magazine and movie I'd ever encountered. The boy I'd chosen was a good-looking upper classman from my high school who'd asked to do one of the most fabled of all dating activities: take me home from school. How could that ever be a bad thing?

Dating was born in the years immediately following the First World War, the time that modern youth culture as we know it was emerging. Thomas Hine, author of *The Rise and Fall of the American Teenager,* describes the twenties as "a society we can easily recognize as a precursor to our own. Although a majority of young people weren't yet in school, there was a widespread belief that they ought to be, and would be soon. Well-developed, truly national news and entertainment media were enraptured by the styles of young people, who were among their most avid watchers.... Young people were, for the first time, setting styles in clothing, hairstyle, music, dancing, and behavior on their own, and both adults and children looked up to them as leaders. Young people were organizing their own social lives, and adults felt powerless when they rejected previous standards of propriety as irrelevant to modern life. Certainly, people in their teens had had fun before, but in the twenties, it became a right."

The war reinvented the very notions of what it meant to be young, and what it meant to be old, or even middle-aged. It opened America's first generation gap. "It was easy," writes

Frederick Lewis Allen in *The Big Change,* for young people "to think of themselves as a generation who had gone through the hell of war because of the mistakes of their elders, whose admonitions on any subject must therefore be suspect." This new feeling of independence and liberation was not reserved only for young men. Wrote Paul Sann in *The Lawless Decade:* "The soldier home from the war did find something to cheer about—unless he happened to be an Honor Scout or other-wise excessive. Johnny found his American beauty drifting away from the prim morality of the pre-1914 world faster than the Model T would carry her.... She wanted to be the life of the party—indoors, or in the open roadster parked on the lonely road.... The curtain had come down on the girl he used to know. She was a flapper now, raring to go." In 1922 *Outlook* magazine ran a piece called "A Flapper's Appeal to Parents": "I wear bobbed hair, the badge of flapperhood. (And, oh, what a comfort it is!) I powder my nose. I wear fringed skirts and bright-colored sweaters, and scarfs, and waists with Peter Pan collars, and low-heeled 'finale hopper' shoes. I *adore* to dance. I spend a large amount of time in auto-mobiles. I attend hops, and proms, and ball-games, and crew races, and other affairs at men's colleges."

This new way of life took off with great speed, in part because the forces of modernity had a running start on the twenties. All of Freud's major theories had been published before the war; Margaret Sanger's campaign to provide ac-cess to contraception was also well under way by 1914. The American teenage girl, completely different from the girls of her mother's generation—and all other previous generations—was a new creature, the product of a convulsive act of youthful self-creation, its tenets broadcast from city to town via all the newly born national culture and the dawn of mass media.

Chief among those media: the movies. Motion pictures, which were seen by millions of Americans every week, including a huge percentage of America's young people, enjoyed the twenties free from the interference of either a Hays Code or a Legion of Decency, both of which would come to power during the artistically reactionary period of the 1930s. As a form of popular entertainment, the movies had emerged not from the concert halls and dramatic stages of America, but from the far seedier world of vaudeville and the boardwalk nickelodeon. Although they soon became a vehicle of middle-class entertainment, for a long while they dealt, in a fairly explicit way, with sexual themes and story lines that had a profound impact on the way young people, and in particular girls, saw themselves and the world around them. We may marvel at the group hysteria of teenyboppers screaming and fainting at the Beatles concert in Shea Stadium, but forty years earlier their counterparts had been brought to a similar frenzy by Rudolph Valentino. Still, there was a significant difference between the two cultural phenomena: the adorable four mop tops represented a kind of sublimated sexuality, to which the girls, in their innocence, felt free to respond. But there was nothing sublimated about Valentino and what he represented. The Sheik inspired the real deal, as the ads for his most famous movie vividly reveal:

SEE

THE AUCTION OF BEAUTIFUL GIRLS TO

THE LORDS OF THE HAREM

SEE

MATCHLESS SCENES OF GORGEOUS COLOR,

AND WILD FREE LOVE IN THE YEAR'S SUPREME

SCREEN THRILL—

3000 IN THE CAST

Girls of the 1920s had a mass-market sex symbol of their own to whom they could aspire—Clara Bow, the original "dirty girl," the slum kid, who begged for money to get her photographs taken for a contest, so she could beam her pretty mug all over the world—an everyday affair for any contemporary American girl with access to a computer. In 1927, she gave girls all across the country a new notion of how to comport themselves. She was the "It" girl, from the movie of the same name, and the "it" in question was what we started to call "sex appeal" by the fifties. As Elinor Glyn, the author of the short story on which the movie was based, would later describe "it": "With 'it' you win all men if you are a woman, all women if you are a man. It can be defined as a quality of the mind as well as a physical attraction." Clara Bow was always getting naked (even if you didn't actually see it on-screen) around men she wasn't married to, and she was racy, wild. She may have shocked a lot of Americans, but in those days the motion picture business was so new, such a Wild West—like the Internet is today—that there was no system in place for policing it.

Clara Bow used her beauty and her sexuality as an aggressive tool for self-promotion; she was the forerunner to Marilyn Monroe, Madonna, Lady Gaga. *It* was about a spunky young shopgirl who sets her cap on the swell who owns the department store, only to find herself fallen into ruin when—for complicated reasons of plot—he discovers her caring for a baby, and assumes it's their love child. Her ability to triumph over all, to continue living a sexually free life, was a revelation to girls who saw the movie by the millions.

Girls' pocket money was a significant force in the development of many of the cultural advances of the decades. An entire material culture developed, one fueled by this pocket money and so aimed especially at teenage girls, including an entirely new kind of consumer product: mass-marketed clothing designed to be worn not by little girls or by grown women. There were "subdeb" boutiques in the big department stores, and specialty shops, as we can see from these two ads printed in Baltimore newspapers in the middle of the decade:

THE TWIXTEEN SHOP

WHERE THE PARTICULAR NEEDS OF MISS
FOURTEEN-TO-TWENTY ARE CAREFULLY STUDIED
AND INTELLIGENTLY PROVIDED FOR.

JOEL GUTTMAN & COMPANY

WHATEVER THE HIGH SCHOOL GIRL NEEDS—

IN APPAREL AND ACCESSORIES—

WILL BE FOUND AT

HOCHSCHILD, KOHN & CO

BALTIMORE'S BEST STORES

HOWARD AND LEXINGTON

Another factor in teenage girls seeing themselves as a distinct and even powerful new class was the emerging concept of adolescence as a separate developmental stage, one that might have challenges and pleasures all its own. It was an idea with roots in psychoanalytic thinking that came to widespread acceptance through the work of an American psychologist named G. Stanley Hall, whose revolutionary 1904 two-volume book on the subject, *Adolescence,* reported that "being a teenager is, in some respects, an unnatural act, an imposition of culture on biology. It means continuing to be a child when your body is telling you otherwise. Young people nearing the peak of their physical and sexual powers are expected to delay using them, and focus their energies on acquiring skills and moral values." In fact it was the twenties— and not the fifties, as much of current popular culture would have us believe—that gave birth to what we mean when we use the term "American teenager": that creature whose life is animated by spending money, a booming peer culture, and the particular social world that emerges through attendance at large coeducational public high schools. Twenties teenagers comprised America's first youth culture, kids who communicated with one another via a private language of slang and gesture, whose indulgent parents saw the teenage years as a time for fun and social activity.

All of these advances both liberated and coarsened the typical American teenage girl, gave her a wide world of prospects her mother never could have imagined for herself, and eroded the various kinds of protections and safeguards that earlier generations of girls had experienced. H. L. Mencken drolly observed in 1916 that "the veriest schoolgirl of today knows as much as the midwife of 1885, and spends a good deal more of her time discharging and disseminating her information." Lloyd Morris remarked of Jazz Age girls in *Incredible New York: High Life and Low Life from 1850 to 1950*, "If your concern was paternal, the flapper was a problem. Otherwise, she was a pleasure. Jauntily feather-footed in her unfastened galoshes, her flesh-colored stockings rolled below the knee and her skirt barely touching it, slender and boyish, the flapper came in to the tune of 'I'll Say She Does'—and frequently she did."

It was within this new world of girl possibility and girl power that dating was born with surprisingly little resistance from parents. As historian Beth L. Bailey reports in her excellent account of the changes in American courtship, *From Front Porch to Back Seat*, the term "dating" was, by 1914, appearing regularly in *Ladies' Home Journal*; by 1924, dating was a widespread practice among middle-class teenagers. The birth of car culture escalated the process; with cars and "parking" came petting, which consisted of any sexual activity short of intercourse and which replaced the much more innocent "spooning" and "snuggle pupping." There was even a body of thought—well documented in a 2007 book called *Female Adolescence in American Scientific Thought, 1830–1930* by Crista DeLuzio—that petting was actually good for girls, that it served a purpose relating to something that only a few years earlier would have been among the most shocking statements you could make: that teenage girls had erotic desires of their own and were not merely the potential victims of adolescent male lust. Phyllis Blanchard, author in 1920 of *The Adolescent Girl,* wrote that so long as the girl was not trading these physical intimacies in the hope of gaining love, but rather wholly to satisfy her own physical desires, the new practice was entirely healthy, even "wholesome....Contrary to a section of popular opinion, she may be better prepared for marriage by her playful activities than if she had clung to a passive role of waiting for marriage before giving in to her sex impulses." G. Stanley Hall wrote that teenage flappers "not only accept, but glory in, their sex as such, and [through petting] are giving free course to its native impulses."

Imagine what had come before: an expectation that a well-raised young woman from a thoughtful and caring family would be absolutely ignorant of sexuality until the night of her wedding, or at least the beginning of her betrothal. For the woman, the act of intercourse, coupled as it was with the act of being uprooted from her home, leaving her mother, being bound to another clan, was an experience that literally penetrated—and violated—her sense of who she was in the world, her safety in her home. There is no shortage of anecdotes and evidence from the historical record to suggest that the experience was very tense, often marked by a combination of ignorance, fear, anxiety. Wedding-night jokes are a lost form of American humor because their very premise—two sexually inexperienced young people intent on losing their virginity—is now so far removed from the reality that their comic shorthand makes no sense. The jokes centered, always, on something going wrong, and it was the woman who had to endure whatever ineptitude or frantic passion her groom brought to the event. To the groom fell either the opportunity for kindness and gentleness or for impatience and cruelty.

In *Education of the Senses,* the first volume of Peter Gay's great exploration of the European and American middle classes from the 1820s to the outbreak of the First World War, he devotes considerable energy to a study of those premodern wedding nights, which he observes are easy to imagine as pure cliché: "The brute in the bedroom, the sensual husband raping his shrinking, wholly uninformed bride, became a staple in the literature of bourgeois self-criticism...it makes for a plausible and—I must add—titillating scene in a melodrama for two: the timid frightened girl torn from the arms of her mother and thrown on the mercy of this man who is her husband."

But in his readings of diaries and letters he found a more nuanced reality. Wedding nights did not uniformly constitute cases of "licensed rape," nor did all middle-class couples arrive at the nuptial chamber in a state of total ignorance, either of human sexuality or—in some cases—of one another's bodies. Not infrequently the period of betrothal, between proposal and marriage ceremony, was a time in which the couple was afforded some privacy, as the young man had already declared his honorable intentions; furthermore, "nineteenth-century bridegrooms were often patient and tactful." Still, the wedding night—"with all its attendant leave-takings" was a hugely emotional and wrenching experience for a girl, made all the more so by her lack of knowledge about her own biology and even about the rudiments of reproduction.

Until the First World War, it was almost impossible for a well-raised girl to get access to the kind of information that would have made for a less anxious wedding night, and whenever someone emerged to provide it, he or she became a person of significant stature. This opened the door to both the helpful and the kooky, and sometimes to people with both traits, such as Ida Craddock, author of *The Wedding Night,* published toward the end of the nineteenth century. Craddock was born in Philadelphia in 1857 and raised in a strict Quaker home. She became the first woman to pass the entrance exams to the University of Pennsylvania, but her enrollment was blocked by the university's trustees. She ended up studying and then teaching at a business college and writing a book on stenography. But in 1887 her life took an unexpected turn: she joined the Theosophist Society and became a student of the occult, eventually proclaiming herself a "priestess and pastor in the church of yoga." She also wrote a series of books and tracts on human sexuality, which offered practical and useful information to readers, especially young and inexperienced ones. As a feminist, she argued persuasively for the encouragement of female erotic desire, but as a person who was admitted five times to psychiatric hospitals, she was prone also to giving advice that was frankly insane and sometimes outright dangerous.

The most famous of her works, *The Wedding Night* was a little pamphlet that explained with great sensitivity the plight of young women on their first night alone with their young husbands, and of the terrifying moment that each bride must face: "It comes when the last kisses of mother and girl-friends have been given, and the last grain of rice has been thrown upon the newly wedded pair, and the last hack driver and hotel or railway porter have been gotten rid of, and the key is turned in the bedroom door and the blinds drawn, and the young girl, who has never been alone in a locked room with a man in all her life, suddenly finds herself, as though in a dream, delivered over by her own innocent and pure affection into the power of a man, to be used at his will and pleasure."

She counsels that in most cases "no genital union at all should be attempted, or even suggested, upon that night," advice that has a long history (even the *Kama Sutra* advises bridegrooms to wait ten days before attempting sex with their new wives), and she tells men that they are not to force their wives into sex. "My dear sir, you must indeed be lacking in manhood to be unable to arouse sex desire in a bride who loves you with even a halfway sort of affection." Fair enough, until you get to this bit of information: "As to the clitoris, this should be simply saluted, at most, in passing, and afterward ignored as far as possible." In fact, Craddock was an advocate, in certain situations, of female circumcision.

But even for girls who had experienced petting before marriage, the wedding night was often their first experience of intercourse, and as such it was often a frightening one. The wedding night described in *Joy in the Morning*, set in 1927, is breathtaking because it is so fully realized and so patently autobiographical. Written by Betty Smith, who became famous for composing one of the most loved novels in all of Girl Land, *A Tree Grows in Brooklyn*, the later book fictionalizes her first year as a very young bride married to a young man studying law at the University of Michigan.

The story opens with Annie—who has just arrived after a long train ride from Brooklyn, and who is eloping—sitting next to her fiancé, Carl, on a wooden bench in the corridor of a town hall, "a small, red, very new suitcase" on the floor beside her.

"Will we have to wait much longer?" Carl asks the clerk anxiously. He is in a hurry; Annie is not.

The wedding takes place, and they arrive at the boardinghouse where they will take up residence, but the room is not yet ready, and there are a series of delays. They sell their tickets to the big football game and use the money for a wedding lunch, then return to the boardinghouse, but still they must wait.

Carl begins to go mad with frustrated passion. First they

had been thwarted by the prying eyes of Brooklyn and the necessities of convention: "All our love-making in public: On the street, in subways, in trolley cars, movies, vestibules.... Always like animals looking for a dark corner." Now, with the marriage license, he has earned his right to a dark corner, but still they sit and sit on the porch swing, waiting. The verandah and the soft air may delight Annie, but her happiness only enrages her new husband.

"I know how you feel, Carl," she says sweetly, "because I feel the same way." But it turns out she does not.

"You don't know," he tells her; "and you don't feel the same. You *can't* know how a man feels. A woman can bide her time and wait. But a man...Me! All keyed up and waiting...waiting all day...waiting years. It's enough to drive a man crazy!"

And then an amazing thing happens; Annie says sympathetically, "I know. Carl, I'll go get a Coke and leave you alone for a few minutes." (Alone to do what?) "Like hell you will," he says, and he grabs her roughly and pulls her on top of him: "He kissed her eyes, her ears, her mouth and the hollow at the base of her neck. He shoved his hand down her blouse and took hold of one of her breasts."

She pleads with him not to do it there on the porch of the respectable house, but her whimpering only angers him: "Fury, added to sexual frustration, made him wild. He grabbed the top of her blouse and tore it down to her waist. The little buttons splattered on the floor. When he began pulling off her jacket, she opened her mouth to scream, but he got his hand over her mouth just in time. She put her two hands on his chest and shoved him out of the swing." The swing then rebounds and clips him, hard, on the knees, and Annie begins to cry.

What a curious scene this is, and how keenly felt by its author—the little buttons spattering on the porch floor a detail so acute and so telling of the changing landscape of this girl's life. And how frightening the moment is because now she is married to this man who—just a few hours earlier, before the marriage—would have been accused of attempted rape if he had done the same thing to her.

As Annie sobs, Carl vows, mysteriously, to "settle this once and for all," and then he stomps inside to insist the landlady give them the room at once. He comes back all smiles: the room will be ready in fifteen minutes, and they are to go to a lunchroom first and have a dinner of sandwiches. "Carl," Annie tells him in a sudden declaration of human rights, "I'm a person that don't like to be grabbed in a swing."

"I'll remember," he says somberly, and then they go back to the boardinghouse and change into their nightclothes. But Annie refuses to have sex. "Because you'll hurt me. I know it."

Finally, miraculously, Carl's heart is moved. Instead of attacking her again, he pulls a chair by the window and asks her to sit in his lap. And then he rocks her like a baby and gently confesses that he's as unschooled as she is: "he told her as much as he knew about the sex act, and she fell asleep in his arms while he was talking." Eventually she wakes up and climbs into bed, and as he hangs his pajama top in the closet he asks her, "If I turn off the light will you take off your night gown?" To which she replies, "It's already off."

It took a husband-and-wife team, the American doctors Hannah and Abraham Stone, who were associates of Margaret Sanger, to write a guidebook that would educate millions of young American women on the facts of sexuality, desire, and the wedding night itself. *Marriage Manual: A Practical Guidebook to Sex and Marriage,* first published in 1936, notes that the new couple needs to get on with things: "It is usually best for the sexual union to be consummated during the first few days after marriage if feasible. If the defloration should prove to be very painful, or if there is much apprehension and fear on the part of the wife, complete penetration need not take place during the first sex act....A gradual and gentle dilation carried out during the several successive relationships will considerably ease the discomfort and lessen the anxiety for the woman." However, the doctors counsel strongly against allowing this period of husbandly patience to outlive its usefulness: "The longer the first relations are postponed the greater will be the feeling of anxiety on the part of the wife and of frustration on the part of the husband." The burden of correcting this situation lay with the wife: "The woman should realize that complete relaxation on her part and an active cooperation are necessary for the consummation of the sexual union."

★ ★ ★

It was from this territory of sexual ignorance and patriarchal courtship that girls of the 1920s began to embrace dating. But no matter how joyously they welcomed the new practice, and how easily their parents and teachers agreed to the new system, there was no denying that it came with a heavy new burden: it was girls' responsibility to set and enforce the standards of how much sexual activity should take place on each date. "Women, according to their nature and in their own best interest," writes Beth Bailey in her book on dating, were the ones who were responsible for setting the sexual limits, for how could dating work otherwise? "If men refused to allow women the power to control their mutual sexual experience," the system could not function. Men were stronger, bigger; the job of controlling what actually took place on dates fell to women — to girls. "No boy — no matter whether he's the head of the Wolf Pack — will persist in affectionate intentions, if he gets a positively negative response," reported the magazine *Senior Scholastic* in 1946. The idea, the one that would many decades later lead me to believe it was okay to go to a deserted beach with a boy I hardly knew, was that any girl — no matter how slight or inexperienced — would be able to control what happened on a date, and if something did go wrong, it was her fault.

As a physical object, the *Seventeen* magazine *Book of Etiquette and Entertaining,* published in 1963, is a beautiful and almost radiantly desirable thing. You can imagine it being given, mother to daughter, as a Christmas or birthday present, the

sort of totem that lets the girl know that her own mother—
however meddlesome and ancient she may seem—is an ally
in the business of being a teenager in the modern world.
It has a sumptuous white dust jacket, with a portrait of a
beautiful girl in a robin's-egg blue hair band, and inside are
chapters on every exciting thing for which an American girl
at midcentury could ever hope. It was written by *Seventeen*'s
founding editor, Enid Haupt, an aging New York heiress with
a passion for horticulture and the French impressionists, for
whom the magazine had been created by her brother, Walter
Annenberg. In the magazine's pages, in the several guidebooks bearing her name, and in her nationally syndicated
newspaper column, Haupt emerges as someone who sees a
girl's teenage years as a training ground for her future as a
young wife, but also as a discrete episode, which—provided
a girl has cultivated the right manners and built the right
wardrobe—should be a career in itself.

The Seventeen Book of Etiquette and Entertaining covers topics ranging from fashion to table manners, party throwing
to partygoing. It was a book written for a mass audience,
but which addressed them—flatteringly—as though they
were all members of a particular upper class, half *Philadelphia Story*, half *Barefoot in the Park*. Yet (and this says as
much about American tastes at midcentury as anything
else) the clear feeling you get from the book is that girls
did not read it as an exercise in social class aspiration, but
as a template of the lives they were in fact living, requir-
ing only a little adjustment. The endless advice on how to

behave in other people's country clubs could be dreamed on and then, with small modifications, applied to the way to conduct oneself during a swim meet at the crosstown Y. And, class aside, the book is filled with things girls wanted to read about: dances and dresses, how to receive a gift of flowers, how to accept an invitation. But most of all— through it all, in the chapters that deal with the subject directly and in the ones that seem to have nothing to do with it directly—it's a book about boys.

On the subject of dating, *The Seventeen Book of Etiquette and Entertaining* is comprehensive, exhaustive. It tells girls how to angle for a date, how to accept a date, how to refuse a date definitively, and how to refuse one yet still keep the door open for a second affair. It tells you what to do if you're wearing the wrong thing for a date, if your young man doesn't have enough money to take you out on a proper date, if you discover that you don't agree with a date's opinions on books or politics. Despite all of these possible blunders, the book still makes dating seem like the most wonderful, exciting, desirable thing that could ever happen to a girl. Yet, mixed in with all of this advice on the fun and romance of dating, there is counsel—sometimes tossed off as an aside, often couched as euphemism, that could easily be missed by a young girl. The core of this advice, although Enid Haupt would almost certainly be loath to put the fact so bluntly, is that dating can be dangerous. Woven pretty tightly within the fabric of the *Book of Etiquette*—and seeming like a subject that doesn't have anything at all to do with what we commonly think of as etiquette—is the recognition of the fundamental power in-equality between teenage boys and girls and the various ways that girls can end up as victims.

There is a section called "How to refuse a kiss," and here, Haupt instructs girls, as they had been instructed since the 1920s, that it is their responsibility to establish how much sex can take place on a date, and furthermore, it is their respon-sibility not to embarrass boys who try for more. "If it's a gay under-the-mistletoe or New Year's kiss, enjoy it and don't stir up a scene over nothing," she tells girls, which on its own is rather shocking advice. If girls find themselves getting a dif-ferent kind of kiss—a "boy-has-plans kind of kiss," she writes that "humor or distraction is the best way to salvage the situ-ation," counsel that struck me because of the word "salvage," as though being kissed in an aggressive way is still a matter of etiquette. But here is the advice that I found chilling, all the more so for the sophisticated, womanly way that it is given: "if one or both of you starts laughing or can be distracted, you can avoid the rather dull feminine response of scratching, screaming and kicking."

I'm not the sort of person who gets worked up over things in guidebooks or newspapers or magazine columns from long ago. But this sentence in the *Seventeen* book stops me every time I read it. This, in essence, was the bill of goods that girls were sold along with dating—we might demand to be allowed to do it, but we'd better be prepared for whatever unpleasant things might take place. We were the ones respon-sible for them.

The hugely popular 1963 book *Love and the Facts of Life* by Evelyn Millis Duvall gives its readers endless fun, peppy advice about how to enjoy a date. "Many dates begin with a boy's asking a girl to go to a special affair with him—a sports event, a musical program, a play," she tells her readers, and each requires a special outfit, a certain kind of planning. Other times the boy asks a girl out for a Saturday night without the foggiest idea of what they should do—in which case the girl should think on her feet, suggesting a double feature or a concert in the park. Keeping conversation rolling on a date can be a challenge, especially for boys who aren't as verbally adept or lively; a girl should work to draw out her date, asking him about his summer plans, courses, after-school activities. But she has another obligation to him: helping him to contain and restrain his sexual urges: down through the ages. It is girls' responsibility to keep relationships between the sexes under control. "On the whole the girls are more slowly aroused and can stop love-making more easily than the average male." How is she going to do this? By making a joke. A girl named Cora, we learn, was out parking with a boy when "his hand slipped down between her breasts and his kiss took on an intensity that was frightening." But Cora had it under control: she "struggled free of his embrace, shook her curls with a jerky little laugh, saying, 'Ooooh please, you are too much for me.'" We're meant to read about this drama in the same breezy way in which it's presented, but I can't: Cora is being manhandled. If she's not resourceful or lucky, she's going to be raped.

As with Enid Haupt's advice on how girls could avoid un-wanted kisses, all of Duvall's counsel regarding this aspect of dating seems steeped in euphemism. You shouldn't let a boy get "fresh" or "take advantage." It seems only to hint, darkly and obscurely, at what life can really be like in a parked car with a boy or young man who turns out not to be such a good guy after all. In fact, the importance of having a date meet your father, which is presented as a point of etiquette, was really another coded message: the father will size him up, intimidate him a bit, let him know that if something goes wrong he won't have just a sixteen-year-old girl to answer to; he will have her father.

The first man to recognize the force of a girl's sexuality is her own father, which is one of the reasons that fatherless girls are always in greater jeopardy. The father is the first line of defense between a girl and the men who would ex-ploit her sexually. Long before she has even entered Girl Land, when she is still blissfully unaware that anyone might have designs on her that run counter to her own best inter-ests, before she has any understanding at all of sexuality, he is nervously watching her, and the men around her, spoil-ing for a fight. The father's job is to protect his girl, and also—during the bittersweet interval in which her sexuality is emerging—to warn her, obliquely as well as directly, of the dark side of male sexuality. When a father gave a daugh-ter "mad money"—a custom still in practice when I was a teenager, at least in my house—he was really warning her, subtly, about the possibility of what we now call "date rape," that even an apparently nice boy can suddenly turn and make demands, force himself on her. Girls with a father living at home always fare better in the dating world, because malevolent adolescent boys (as opposed to the many good ones) don't want to come up against the authority of grown men. In fact, the hallmark of most dangerous teenage boys is that they have never been held to account by a grown man, and they move more confidently in a world of women, where they can threaten and cajole.

All of the dating guidebooks from the twenties until fairly recently make it clear that a girl must introduce her date to her father before she goes out with him, and that if she doesn't have a father, she should introduce him to some older male family member. The guidebooks made this seem like a point of etiquette, but it was really another of the quiet safety mechanisms built into the system: the boy should not leave the house with the girl until he has had to confront the person of her father. Even today, we see dads wanting to be involved in their daughter's teenage romances. Rule 4 of W. Bruce Cameron's *8 Simple Rules for Dating My Teenage Daughter,* an open letter to potential suitors, informs young men interested in his girl, "I'm sure you have been told that in today's world, sex without using a 'barrier method' of some kind can kill you. Let me elaborate: when it comes to sex, I am that barrier, and I will kill you." This little speech would have more resonance if he'd delivered it to his daughter. She is the one, of course, who will make the decisions about how far to take her sexual relationship, but the notion harkens back to something older, and is embedded into the very notion of dating.

I never told anyone what had happened to me that afternoon at the beach. I had been so glad to get home unharmed, so ashamed of what had almost happened, that it seemed like a dark secret that I should never share. A few months later I started dating a nice boy who became my boyfriend for the rest of senior year, and then I went away to college. The summer after sophomore year at college, I got a job working at a department store on Long Island. It was an especially good and fun job, working in the men's shirts department; my boss loved me, the hours were excellent, and I had money of my own. One day, when I was standing at my glass counter (wearing a pink shirtdress, which I remember thinking was both very cute and exactly the right thing for a young woman working in the men's shirts department), I became aware of a young man walking toward me; I glanced up and saw that he had turned his back and was walking away, and I went back about my business. But a few minutes later, in my peripheral vision, I saw the same young man headed toward me, purposeful, single-minded, determined. It was the boy who had forced himself on me at Cedar Beach.

I felt differently about myself then: I had made friends, I had gone to college and had yet another boyfriend; I was much more sure of myself. I certainly wasn't afraid. I was standing on the fluorescent-lit sales floor of Abraham and Straus at ten in the morning. But I braced myself; what was he about to do to me? When he got closer, I realized he was shaking, and when he got all the way to the counter I saw that he was nearly crying.

"I just always wanted to tell you I'm sorry," he said, in a desperate, urgent way. "I'm sorry about what I did to you."

I was so unprepared for the moment, so eager for it to end, that I sort of batted my hand away as though it had been no big deal. I said some idiotic thing like "Oh, don't worry about it." But he wouldn't go away, and he was clearly overcome with his guilt. "I'm just really, really sorry," he said again while I stood there uncomfortably. He was like the date raper of apologizing! He was going to force that apology on me whether I wanted it or not.

Many years later, I was able to view him, and his embarrassing moment in the department store, with a bit of compassion. Between the moment he had tried to assault me and the one in which he came to me in tears, he had realized that he had done something terrible. Like me, he had been only a teenager, after all. It must be a sobering thing for a young man of his age to realize what he was capable of doing.

It really seemed as if he wanted something else from me that day at A and S, but I couldn't figure out what it was, and I certainly didn't feel beholden to him in any way, so I finally just turned from him and busied myself with something else, and he was forced to go back to where he came from, and I never saw him again.

CHAPTER THREE

Menstruation

GIRLS' ATTITUDES TOWARD MENSTRUATION—and toward what it signifies: their budding sexuality—have changed profoundly in the past seventy-five years, and a principal reason for this change is that in the modern world, pregnancy and childbirth are unlikely to result in a woman's death. This might seem a strange source of reassurance for an eleven- or twelve-year-old girl, but for most of human history being closer to reproduction put a girl closer to death, and the bittersweet feelings with which mothers often greeted their daughters' first periods had to do with that horrifying truth of the female condition.

Today, girls often anticipate menstruation with excitement, as a marker of the coming glamour of the teen years. Yet menstruation is still something to be reckoned with; it reveals to girls in a stark and euphemism-free way that they are designed to bear the brunt of sexuality in ways boys and men are not. A girl in early adolescence is eager to begin the life of dating and romance that she has been dreaming about for years, even as a very small child. Why do so many little girls love to pretend they are princesses? They are attracted to the romance, just as they are attracted to stories about weddings and new families, just as they love to play with baby dolls and imagine themselves as little mothers. Dating, romance, having a baby of her own—these are thrilling concepts to a little girl, who has no idea about the complex questions of sexuality and men that must be reconciled before she can begin to experience them. Realizing that before the dating and the romance have even begun, her body is already preparing itself to carry and bear a child, is sobering. All the cheerful Tampax ads in the world—the pretty teenage girls running on the beach, smiling and confident as boys look on admiringly—can't change the truth of menstruation. The makers of sanitary products, as well as teachers and doctors and nurses, have spent a lot of time over the past seventy-five years giving menstruation a makeover, but the experience reveals some deep truths that each girl must come to terms with on her own, and this gathering understanding is part of the important work of Girl Land.

* * *

Menstruation has evolved from being thought of as a dark and potentially dangerous event (for centuries there was a widespread belief in Western cultures, right up to fifty years ago in this country, that if a girl caught a chill while having her period it might kill her) to one that has been aligned with the sunny advertising of the consumer culture directed at teenage girls. Before the modern era, menstruation, along with most aspects of women's reproductive health, was a somewhat mysterious function; it was not until the 1930s that its exact relationship to ovulation and pregnancy was fully understood in scientific terms. Before then, beliefs about menstruation, and particularly about the ways a girl should be instructed about her period, were grounded in tradition and superstition, foremost among them that for the first year or two after a girl begins her period, she needed to stay close to her mother, even dropping out of school for the interlude. In the influential nineteenth-century book for parents *Sex in Education,* Edward Clarke expressed the attitude that was common in middle-class America at that time: "One rule should be absolute in every home. The mother should keep her daughter with her, and near her, until the turning point between childhood and girlhood is safely passed and regularity of habits is established." It was believed that during those first few years mothers and daughters had a need for one another, an emotional symbiosis, in which the mother could feel safe knowing that she alone was educating her child on the proper ways of conducting herself, not only during her menstrual periods, but during her emerging life as a sexual being.

These were attitudes that began to change after the First World War, as a raft of recent social histories, among them *The Modern Period* by Lara Freidenfelds, explain. The advance of medical knowledge, the emerging attitude that the public interest was served by educating Americans about sexuality and reproductive health, and the development and mass marketing of consumer products that made the management of one's period something that was not onerous, even easy, all worked together to bring about this change. As Freidenfelds writes, almost everything we think and do regarding menstruation is the product of a relatively recent set of ideas and innovations. The kind of lives that modern girls and women wanted to pursue "entailed work, school, and recreational situations that demanded a new level of attention to self-preservation and personal efficiency.... The popular conception of a 'modern' way to handle menstruation incorporated new social, cultural, and economic patterns that historians recognize as central to American modernity."

Among these new girl desires was the wish to be away from home as much as possible, and chief among the requirements for doing that was finding a clean, convenient, and dependable way to handle periods. Sanitary napkins (as opposed to the ghastly cloth diapers that had to be boiled clean on the stovetop) had been available—via catalogue order—as early as the late 1800s, but it wasn't until the 1920s that a "culture of disposability" was born, whereby the notion of purchasing an item for the express purpose of sullying it and then getting rid of it was something a large number of girls and women were willing and economically able to do. When the pads were introduced on a large scale by the Kotex Company in 1920, the timing was right, and within a short time they became the norm for American women and girls. Sanitary napkins became essential in the creation of the twentieth-century ideal of the modern body, one that was "well-controlled," writes Freidenfelds, and that did not "leak, smell, or hurt."

At the same time, doctors and scientists were beginning to better understand the function and purpose of menstruation, and suddenly girls began learning about the subject in a new setting and context. The national interest in improving public education about health and hygiene, one of the hallmarks of the Progressive Era, meant that schoolchildren were increasingly being taught a second curriculum, along with academics, this one dedicated to personal cleanliness and habits, from how to brush their teeth and eat a balanced diet, to—eventually—the facts and management of menstruation. Instructing girls about how to take care of this intimate aspect of their private lives was a role taken away from their mothers and sisters and filled instead by paid teachers, and put into the semipublic context of a classroom. It was a breathtakingly huge change in the private lives of girls and women, and it happened rapidly, beginning shortly after the First World War and almost fully realized by the 1950s. The arrival of the first period was transformed from a deeply private experience that brought a young girl into an interlude of intense closeness with her own mother, to a subject thoroughly addressed in the public education system and comprising an essentially hygienic matter that had to be managed in a "sanitary" manner, with the primary emphasis being on keeping one's clothing unstained and one's body sweet-smelling.

During this process, public schools partnered—in an unprecedented alliance—not with the mothers and families of the girls, but with the manufacturers of commercial goods, who were eager to provide classroom content as a means of establishing brand preference from a young age. During the Second World War, many of the big American movie studios had produced educational films for GIs, earnest little one-reelers on everything from how to clip their toenails to how to avoid getting gonorrhea in a foreign port city; when the war was over, these same studios turned toward the production of similar films for use in schools. And so it was that one of the century's most influential American movies was *The Story of Menstruation,* a short animated film made by the Walt Disney studio "through the courtesy of Kotex products." Millions of American girls saw it, and its central premise—a stroke of brilliance on the part of Kotex—was that by aligning menstruation not with the vaguely medical world of earlier advertising campaigns and lesson plans (which often featured nurses and hazy threats about the "unpleasant odor" of menstruation) but rather with the newly emerging teen culture—the one that imagined the American high school girl living in a dreamy world of malt shops and prom dates, saddle shoes and corsages—they could make the purchase of sanitary products exciting and fun and glamorous.

The Story of Menstruation sells the experience as if it were the most enchanted, fantastical thing ever. Its protagonist is as lovely and doe-eyed and long-lashed as any Disney princess. We meet her first as an adorable baby in a frilly bassinet and watch her transform into a beautiful young girl in a filmy buttercup yellow dress. But—the enduring and inescapable problem with approaching the subject from this perspective—the actual content of the film was as jarring and un-Disney-like as you could get: one minute girls were identifying with the beautiful heroine, watching her chat with her bevy of friends, and the next minute they were being shown a medical chart of the female reproductive system and being told about the lining of blood, the possibility of a fertilized egg getting stuck in a fallopian tube, the monthly, bloody shedding of the unused lining. *The Story of Menstruation* has the same problem as all of the other cultural products intended to make menstruation seem fun: it has to skip right over the dating and the dressing up and the first call from a boy and go straight to the truth about female reproduction, pregnancy, and the reality that having your period doesn't really signal that you're ready for a real-life Mystery Date. It signals that you are now ripe to be mated with, to reproduce.

A girl's first period is an event that brings with it—both for her and her mother—a wide spectrum of emotions, some of them bittersweet. These are the feelings that are bound up in menstruation and its connection to several dark mysteries of womanhood, ones with which the average girl in early adolescence has no interest in acquainting herself, but which—

from that point forward—she can never truly evade. In *My Little Red Book,* a 2009 compilation of stories about girls' first periods, we find this unease expressed over and over again. A contemporary girl who gets her first period while on a trip to Paris with her mother—a trip on which she had previously been a real little snot—throws her arms around her mom, grateful for the comfort at this important moment: "Mommy, I love you sooo much." But her mother's words of reassurance fall short of the job: "'Now you'll be able to have a baby,'" she tells her thirteen-year-old, "which didn't make me feel any better." And, as a *New York Times* reviewer of the collection notes, one astounding thing about it is the way that so many girls who were comprehensively educated and carefully prepared for their first periods, girls who were actually excited about getting it, find blood in their underwear and think they are dying. Menstrual blood is real blood, and the process that it heralds is very different from the romanticized vision of younger girls.

Despite the deeper truths at the heart of menstruation, the makeover machine kept going, producing, in 1970, perhaps its greatest achievement, a book that changed my life and the lives of millions of other girls who read it. Judy Blume's novel *Are You There God? It's Me, Margaret* represents the apogee of the notion that menstruation was nothing more or less than an exciting and superfun part of being a teen.

Judy Blume, who has sold more than seventy-five million copies of her twenty-plus novels and who has been awarded the National Book Foundation's Medal for Distinguished Contribution to American Letters, is one of the most banned writers in America. Born in 1938, she married young, established housekeeping in suburban New Jersey, and promptly had two children. She loved the kids but loathed the housewifery, and as a creative outlet she took a class in children's literature.

Blume describes her childhood as one in which she was "dying with curiosity" about sex, but there was nowhere in the 1940s and 1950s for a nice girl to get any information. The memory of that burning curiosity led her to write a novel about a twelve-year-old waiting to get her period, *Are You There God? It's Me, Margaret*. Before the publication of this subversive work, a bookish girl interested in the emotions and practicalities surrounding menstruation would be nudged by a sympathetic teacher toward Anne Frank's *Diary of a Young Girl*, which does address the subject with candor, but the general mood of the book—what with the Holocaust and all—did not generate much enthusiasm for the menses. The dearest book of my childhood, Betty Smith's *A Tree Grows in Brooklyn*, includes Francie's first period, but again, the novel's no upper: shortly after first blood Francie is assaulted by a pervert in a tenement hallway. At twelve I knew a few basic facts about menstruation—it somehow involved babies and shedding a lining and blood everywhere—gleaned in one of the ancient ways (my older sister pulled me into her bedroom one night after dinner and gave me a lecture I'll never forget) and was possessed by an unholy fear of it.

And then I went to Naomi Zimmerman's birthday party, and while the other girls slumbered through the night, I stayed up and read one of the presents, a brand-new copy of *Are You There God? It's Me, Margaret*. By dawn I was a new girl. Here was a character on the brink of getting her first period, and she wasn't frightened or anxious or even ambivalent about this fact—she couldn't wait. A revelation.

Reading *Are You There God? It's Me, Margaret* for the first time in thirty years meant realizing anew that the world of my childhood is as distant and unrecoverable as that of the Etruscans. Margaret and I were young during a time when little girls dreamed of getting the courage to ask their mothers for training bras, attended carefully supervised dances, eagerly wore clothes that the modern preteen would sooner die than put on. ("Should I wear my velvet?" Margaret asks her mother when she learns she's been invited to a boy-girl supper party. "It's your best," her mother replies.) In Margaret's world the boys can't be counted on to maintain a grown-up demeanor for these events: they disappoint the girls by stomping on their toes during a PTA-sponsored square dance; at the supper party they throw their sport coats in a pile and shoot mustard at the ceiling through drinking straws. But it is also the boys who are responsible for introducing the first glimmerings of sex to the group. When a boy suggests that they turn off the light and play Guess Who—"the boys line up on one side and the girls on the other and then when I yell *Go* the boys run to the girls' side and try to guess who's who by the way they feel"—the girls put on the brakes immediately. ("'No, thank you,' Gretchen said. 'That's disgusting!'") The girls agree to a game of Spin the Bottle, however, and that night Margaret gets her first thrilling, fleeting kiss. The novel ends in triumph: three drops of blood on Margaret's underpants, discovered the day of the sixth-grade farewell party, mean that she has left childhood behind.

Through all of these events Margaret's parents are by her side, helping her negotiate her excitement and her fears, congratulating her on each of the steps she makes toward womanhood. I've read many books that changed my life, many books that made such a deep and immediate impression on me that I remember their covers in the vivid way that you remember images from dreams. But nothing ever bore into me the way *Are You There God? It's Me, Margaret* did. Sitting up all night, as around me the other eleven- and twelve-year-old girls slept and stirred and murmured in their sleeping bags, I felt as though I were receiving the secret knowledge I hadn't even known I was looking for, that I'd been so deeply worried about something that I didn't even realize how anxious I was until the fear abated. It was going to be all right.

It *was* all right. But it was not, even after all of that instruction and cheerleading and secret knowledge, at all like what I had been expecting. In the first place, menstrual blood didn't look anything like I thought it would. Although I never saw *The Story of Menstruation* as a girl, its approach to the fluid—which it presents as snowy white—was somewhat in line with what I'd had in mind. All of the accoutrements of menstruation that I had seen around the house—the pale blue and white boxes of Tampax; the pink plastic compacts that came tucked inside them for carrying two tampons discreetly in your purse; that the name of the pads, Modess, which sounded so much like "modest"—implied that although the word "blood" was alarming, the actual fluid would not be. The pink plastic compacts suggested that menstruation was part of the exciting, alluring world of being a teenager: training bras with pink appliqué roses sewn between the cups, half-slips, nylons, hot rollers, boy-girl dances. Kissing, dating, cars—boyfriends! It couldn't happen soon enough. Menstruation ("getting your period" it was called, making it seem an acquisition like any other: "getting" your Bare Trap platform sandals, "getting" your own Princess telephone) was so essentially and centrally a part of that desired, imagined, longed-for world that it couldn't be as bad, as messy or strange or shocking, as the basic fact of blood (*blood?*) suggested.

My best friend got her period before I did, and she seemed afterward to gather into herself, to have some kind of quietness about her, a distance. Her parents had recently bought themselves a new bedroom set, meaning that Naomi now had their old double bed. It was the one we used to lie on as little girls when we watched *The Odd Couple* in her parents' bedroom on Friday nights, while her mom sat next to us, folding laundry. I remember some of the happiest nights of my childhood sitting on that bed. Now it was Naomi's, as though since she started menstruating the house itself had offered up a totem of sexuality and reproduction. Boys called her on the telephone, she had Carly Simon's *No Secrets* propped against the wall underneath her window; she seemed the same but different.

And then—on a Sunday morning, when my parents and I had tickets to see a matinee performance of the San Francisco Ballet, three hours to be spent sitting on the crushed red velvet seats of the opera house—it came. And it was blood. Real blood. Rust brown once it dried, viscous and shiny when it was fresh, not altogether free of horrible little clots and clumps. When you pulled down your underpants—so carefully chosen from the girls department at Penney's, with the elastic lace and the flower print—there it was, the pad: a horror. Ghastly. The gore of it, the smell of it. You were expected to go to school—bleeding. And have slumber parties—bleeding. Clearly, it was not really the logical extension of your frilly little-girl room, the way hot rollers and half-slips were the logical extension of that magical space. My Barbie dolls had half-slips and rollers. They didn't have bandages of warm, malodorous blood strapped between their legs. Every little girl has spent hours factoring romance and boyfriends and sweetly dressed babies into her future, but the rude, bloody truth of female reproduction has never occurred to her until it shows up, wanted or not, waited for or dreaded: the first eviction notice from little girlhood. In primitive cultures they take girls away for a month to get used to the idea. Why just a month? Why not a decade? Why not forever? This blood, this truth: the truth of childbearing and of a womb relentlessly preparing itself for the implantation of a fertilized egg—this was going to take some getting used to. I was going to have to come to terms with it.

Menstruation, no matter how much it is sanitized and re-branded, signifies that a girl is coming of age sexually—not just to the boys at school she likes and wants to notice her, but also to the much larger world of men, who begin to take an increasing sexual interest in her as she matures. That a sexually budding adolescent girl becomes the sudden object of predatory male attention has been the cause of parental anxiety down through the ages. When I was a young teenager in 1973, the horror movie *The Exorcist* took America by storm. It was a supernatural tale of the occult, but it also had within it a central idea that was at once culturally relevant and deeply terrifying: that as soon as a young girl came of sexual age, she became vulnerable to a new class of danger.

In several respects, *The Exorcist*—which both stands up over time and looks more ridiculous than ever—was a seventies story. As Mark Kermode later observed of its phenomenal success, "For the first time in a mainstream movie, audiences witnessed the graphic desecration of everything that was considered wholesome and good about the fading American Dream—the home, the family, the church and, most shockingly, the child." The household at the movie's center is not a happy one. The father is absent, and the mother, who is a movie star, clearly has a complicated sexual life, which no child would relish. She and her daughter, Regan, have no real home, moving from one film location to another and depending on a personal assistant to care for them. The event begins, as the old Roman Catholic doctrine says that it will, with an "infestation," a series of scuffling noises in the attic, assumed to be rats. And then the possession begins, and its predominant nature is sexual. *The Exorcist* was a movie of its time: it confronted one of the major social anxieties of the 1970s. Divorce was creating so many fatherless households, which left a new generation of middle-class daughters without a man to protect them from sexual opportunists. And the film raises the specter of a polluted and depraved sexuality that might inhabit such a child, the same kind of sexuality that was the center of a later movie, *Hardcore,* in which a well-raised teenage daughter suddenly and implausibly disappears into the world of pornography. In *The Exorcist,* Regan starts out as the sweetest, most loving little girl on the planet, and then she turns twelve, and a monster takes hold of her. What might be a gently unfolding sexual awakening becomes a horrifying, bloody, and violating event.

For years, there was a series of jokes about the movie that traded on the notion of the perplexed mother saying to Regan, "What's gotten into you?" This was the question that propelled the movie into something larger than the sum of its parts. When a little girl begins her slow disappearing act, it breaks her mother's heart. The arrival of the period—the last breath of her true childhood—is like the two-minute warning, the last chance for teddy bear teas and the romantic fascination with her mother as the summa of all things feminine. When the sunny daughter who once stood on the stepping stool helping her mother cut out cookies becomes the sulking mocker, Mom feels as though an abduction has taken place. It's Persephone all over again, except that instead of the aching absence of the abducted daughter, a wretched changeling is left behind, at once similar to the vanished girl, and her poisonous opposite.

The Exorcist trades on a fact that we don't like to admit to ourselves: that with menstruation, a little girl doesn't just transform into a somewhat—or even significantly—older girl. Menarche lurches her, no matter how far behind her emotional and psychological development may lie, into a creature capable of being impregnated. All over the world, and quite often here in the United States, there are girls as young as twelve who give birth because some man took a look at them and thought they were worth his time sexually, and the next thing you know, a girl who hasn't even reached her full height or shoe size, who is hardly old enough to attend a PG-13 movie, is growing a second human within her slight body. She is vulnerable to the sexual power and force of men as well as to the terrible consequences of that sexuality. It is these realities, ultimately, that make *The Exorcist* so terrifying. Before menarche, a girl is prey only to the sexual attention of the psychiatrically disturbed. Pedophiles are as thin on the ground as they are terrifying. But with menstruation, and the sexual unfolding that comes with it, a daughter becomes a sexually appropriate object of male desire long before she becomes a socially appropriate one. The devil would never have entered the body of a six-year-old girl; he wants one with whom he can mate.

* * *

Girls are forced to confront the sexual attention of men from the beginning of their adolescence, a major reason why female adolescence is so much more emotionally intense than male adolescence. It is also one of the reasons why girls are so much more voluble than boys. Go anywhere there are young adolescent girls in groups, and what you will discover is a word made flesh: embarrassment has become not merely an arrangement of letters signifying a particular emotional state; it has been rendered into squeals, blushes, bodies bent over in gales of laughter because laughter—irrepressible and contagious—is the only physical response as intense as the stimulus itself. Go up to a group of girls ordering Iced Blendeds at the Coffee Bean, and ask one of them a simple question, the kind that strangers often ask one another. Ask her what time it is, or if she has already ordered, or whether you can reach past her to pick up a copy of the *New York Times* from the rack beyond her. She will look at you blankly, as though stunned, for a moment or two, and then she will begin to answer. In short order, things are likely to go wrong. The other girls will notice that she has come to your attention, and they begin to graze one another's bony rib cages with poking elbows, and there is a cascading effect, a great spilling of dominoes— girl after girl—that ends with the one you've queried, and then she's useless. She's as red-faced and giggly as if you'd just shown her a naked picture. Everyone finds this behavior off-putting. One of the forces that protect teenyboppers from older teenage boys is the fact that many of them can't be bothered to penetrate the charged embarrassment. Adults who are generally charmed by young girls and also beguiled by older, self-contained teenage girls will look away when they see these girls. They make us uncomfortable, in part because we feel embarrassed for them.

Boys the same age aren't like this at all. They are easily chagrined, of course, and they face their own moments of epic humiliation, often involving sports or the hazards of public shaming that constitute a typical day in a boys' locker room. But when twelve- and thirteen-year-old boys travel in packs through a mall or a skate park, they are rarely concerned with their effect on others, and if asked for the time of day or the location of an Amoeba Music store, a boy will answer the question as quickly and forthrightly as he can, in order to get away from the adult, whose interests are unlikely to merge with his own.

And this, precisely, is the difference between men and women, made manifest in the pubescent children who are beginning on the path to adulthood. The reason girls are so often embarrassed is that they are so keenly aware of the impression they are making, which is to say that they are keenly, at times unbearably, sensitive to the presence and the emotional state of others. Ultimately, this overly acute sensitivity to the feelings of others will mellow and transform itself into one of the natural graces of womankind: empathy, kindness. When you are experiencing some small moment of social discomfort, how often is it a woman who notices and rescues you—shows you the table on which to set down your party gift, draws attention to your pretty necklace when you're miserable for having underdressed, tells a story of her child's lowest moment when yours is screaming on the supermarket floor?

The first time a man whistles at a girl from afar or blasts his horn as he's driving past her—these firsts are puzzling to girls, who don't quite understand them in the beginning. The attention feels threatening, unexpected, inexplicable. Why is that grown-up honking at me? What am I doing wrong? It takes time and experience to realize that these men, strangers, are reacting impulsively to the girl's sexuality. The man honking that horn might be a perfectly nice guy, he might never act on that desire, even if the recipient of his attention ran up to him and begged him to take her somewhere private. But he honked that horn to say: you have sent a signal to me, either through your clothes or your manner, or simply through the very fact that you have come of age, that you are available to be seen and fantasized about as a sexual creature.

By the time a girl is twenty, she will know how to endure these moments without being frightened; by the time she's thirty, she might even enjoy them; and by the time she's forty, she will start to miss them. But when she's fourteen, fifteen, sixteen—these are occasions of shock and fear and also, gradually, of excitement, proof of her effect on men. No matter how checked that impulse might be by the forces of decency, propriety, convention, or custom, it swirls around the girl, landing on her many a day. The girl's gathering awareness of this fact—and her sensitivity to when that energy constitutes something essentially benign and perhaps even flattering, and when that energy is threatening and possibly even danger-ous—is one of the great hallmarks of the passage from Girl Land to womanhood.

The fourteen-year-old babysitter who is driven home, late, by a tipsy father who has dropped his familiar, long-con-quered wife back home with the babies and the pets, and is now free, on the open road, with a young girl. The great-uncle who wants the niece to sit on his lap all night—not just during dessert, but while the family is gathered in the living room, while *The Lion King* beams out yet again from the tele-vision, who holds her tight—confines her, traps her there—when she would rather sit on her own, with her brothers, on the floor. How many moments are there in life when that sex-ual energy, awakened in a man, falls (but is not acted upon, necessarily, and not always obvious even to himself) upon a young girl? "You're too old for that now," a mother will say sharply when she comes upon her eleven-year-old daughter snuggled with Daddy on the rec room couch, and the signif-icance of her words come like a shock, and he moves away from the daughter, never to be that physically affectionate with her again. It is a loss to the girl, she doesn't understand it, except in a vague and troubling way. It has something to do with sex, she understands. It is a disturbing, troubling new time of her life, and menstruation is when it begins.

Historically, the passage out of Girl Land was so much more poignant than the one out of little boyhood because it was a preparation for death. Those days, for those of us in the first world, are mostly over, but it was a truth for so much of human existence — and still is, in many places — that the cultural residue, the holdover of feelings and sentiment, the way we regard the coming of menstruation, hasn't completely caught up with that fact.

Jerry Seinfeld used to have a routine about the television commercials for laundry detergents that promise the product will remove bloodstains from clothing. "I think if you've got a T-shirt with bloodstains all over it," Seinfeld would say, "maybe laundry isn't your biggest problem." It's a funny line, and it's one that only a man could think of, because the real reason that blood is such a vexing and eternal laundry problem doesn't have to do with gunshot wounds or serial shaving mishaps (in the commercials, a witless husband is forever nicking himself shaving, usually wearing his best white shirt, the male equivalent of showering in your bra and panties). Bloodstains occur and recur in households because women spend a lot of their lives bleeding. If a man or a child woke up in a small pool of blood, the alarm would be genuine and well founded. But if a woman does so, it's business as usual. The bloodiness of menstrual blood is something that has been steadily de-emphasized in the past century, but blood it surely is. I once walked into the students' restroom at an all-girls school late in the afternoon on a warm day, and the smell that assailed me was singular and unmistakable: blood.

Every month, a woman's womb slowly fills with blood in anticipation of an event that she wants to occur only a few times at most, and that up until seventy years ago had a good chance of killing her. This is nature's unkind way with women. The sort of man who knocks a woman up and then disappears is nowhere near as heartless as nature, which allows a fertilized egg to implant in a fallopian tube, or arranges a baby's body in the womb in such a way that it cannot by any natural means escape through the birth canal, or spreads the placenta across the cervix so that it will rupture and cause a hemorrhage almost certain to kill the mother if no medical staff is on hand to stop it. That modern medicine has so radically reduced the incidence of death in childbirth testifies less to advances in science than to the crudeness of the dangers at hand. Menstruation reveals to girls the complexity of the female condition and the ways in which, unlike boys, their bodies have been designed not just for the pleasure of sexuality, but also for the consequences of sexuality. Leaving Girl Land requires coming to terms with that truth.

CHAPTER FOUR

Diaries

CITIZENS OF GIRL LAND are strongly attracted to diary-keeping. It is an act that requires retreat from the world and the quiet examination of one's interior life, and so it is entirely consistent with some of the most profound female impulses—to live deeply in one's emotions, to examine not just one's thoughts but also one's feelings. Diaries also provide a private, protected space for a girl to explore an emerging new self, to try on personas—of jaded sophistication, of mawkish innocence, of unleashed anger—as she faces the task of leaving Girl Land behind and becoming a woman. Although diaries, with their little padlocks and carefully hidden keys, are meant to be secret, safeguarded from prying eyes, there is always within them an element of performance, a sense that they are being written for an audience. Because for a teenage girl, writing a diary is an act of becoming someone new, and the diary is the place where the new public persona makes its first experimental appearances.

"Diaries," writes Joan Jacobs Brumberg in *The Body Project*, "reveal so much about the heart of being a girl...providing generations of girls with a way to explore or express those feelings." The diaries she cites often revolve around a set of themes: friendships and crushes, the process of breaking away from home and family, changing bodies. Girls' fads and trends change through time, but "unlike samplers and embroidering, adolescent diaries persist, providing generations of girls a way to express and explore their lives and feelings." A diary is a place where a girl can record and examine her sexual progress, sometimes written in code, sometimes in the most frank and unambiguous language. Girls write about their intimate moments with boyfriends; the sexual advances, demurrals, and acceptances; the pleasure sex brings and the worry it engenders. Brumberg describes a girl's diary from the 1860s, when the writer "kept company" with a young man named Henry who would eventually fight in the Civil War, and whose kisses she made note of with an asterisk. "After tea," reads one entry, she and Henry "went into the parlor, shut the door and had a visit. He tried to sleep in my lap, but couldn't. Had such a good time." But here the entry fades into a few ecstatically wiggly lines followed by the simple, enigmatic, and charged word "buttons." A girl diarist from the fifties described a date with her boyfriend that makes clear the extent to which diary prose often reflects the kind of popular culture in which the authors are immersed: "His lips were on mine, hard and pressing and insistent, making my head fall back....I never knew a kiss could be like that." Reflecting on this powerful moment, she writes—in a phrase so innocent it's heartbreaking—"Now I am a woman." What she means, certainly, is that the urgent kiss had been coupled with the force of male sexuality, and with her own matching desire, the powerful combination of the two giving her reason to see herself as no longer just a girl. Always, the teenage girl is coming to terms with the difference between romance as she imagined it when a child—a world of swirling dresses and boys whose affections were almost paternal in their chasteness—to the reality of sexual need, desire, conquest, and danger.

The impulse to relive a date in a secret journal seems to be an overwhelmingly feminine one. I can't imagine a boy dropping a girl home the night of his first sexual experience and thinking to himself, "I've got to get home before I forget a single second of this. I need to record every moment in my diary!" But how many thousands, how many millions of girls, have walked into their rooms and reached behind the other books in the bookcase so that they could begin—through the act of private writing and reflecting—to document, savor, and understand what has happened?

Keeping a diary is like closing your bedroom door and refusing to come out until dinnertime: it is a declaration of self.

The teenager is entering new territory and her parents cannot accompany her on the journey. Mothers are desperate to be involved in this passage—they've made it themselves, of course, and they would do anything to steer their daughter the right way. It is frustrating beyond measure for them when a daughter screams, "You don't understand, and you'll never understand!" The mother stamps her foot in aggravation, but in this case the daughter is right: the mother doesn't understand. She merely remembers, and memory is separate from experience. Half the fights in a household containing a teenage girl are based on this simple truth. A daughter can take all of her new feelings, among them this strange new sense of separateness from her mother, to her diary. In it, she takes her first, tentative steps toward an identity separate from her parents, and from the home that has a vested interest in remembering the little girl who once lived within this burgeoning adolescent.

This is why diaries have always been so interesting and so tempting to mothers, and why their contents have so often been shocking to them: they are desperate to find out everything about their daughters, to tear down the new wall that separates them so cruelly. Of all the important aspects of diary-keeping, perhaps the least understood but most universal is the diary's role in helping a girl to make a break from her mother. The fights and sulks and screaming matches that mark a household occupied by a teenage girl and her middle-aged mother are part of this necessary process, but the seeds of it are sown, often, in the diary, which is where the girl first experiments with criticizing her mother, who until the pre-teen years had seemed like a beacon of pure goodness and matchless femininity. The modern mother is motivated, in her relationship with her teenager, to know everything that is going on. Every generation of kids is up to new things, pulling off new stunts, getting away with things that the last generation could not have imagined. To the parents of girls, this seems especially dangerous and troubling, and the diary—so tempting, so brimming with lush narrative descriptions of the very things the mother is trying to learn about—can seem like the Rosetta stone of daughters.

One of the central jobs of all adolescents is to make a break from their parents, and for girls this comes in the form of the sudden, violent realization that her mother is an absolute burden, the pure antithesis of everything she wants for herself, who she wants to become. What more primal moment is there, in the relationship of an adolescent daughter and her mother, than the one in which Mom violates the diary and learns something she hadn't known, or had suspected but of which she had no proof? Sometimes the mother seethes with the knowledge for days—or forever—because she is too embarrassed to admit how she has come to be in possession of it. When I was a high school teacher and guidance counselor I several times had mothers contact me to fret about something they had read in a daughter's diary (along with the convoluted stories they felt it was necessary to tell me about how they had come across the diary, how the thing had sort of fallen open in front of them, when clearly they had been reading it for quite some time, or at the very least had made it the target of a calculated commando raid). Everything is wrong with the mother, you learn in a diary: her hair, her clothes, her preoccupations, her well-intentioned bits of counsel about teenage life. All of this pent-up anger is as fleeting as adolescence itself; most girls end up, in one way or another, very much like their mothers. But during puberty a daughter must create not just a new relationship with her mother but also, in a sense, a new self. Often the diary is the first place she goes to create this new self and new relationship.

The most famous girl diary of all time, Anne Frank's, was written not merely as a letter to herself but also with an eye toward an audience, in her case a specific one. That *The Diary of a Young Girl* was partly the secret record of an adolescent girl's private emotional life during a harrowing event, yet also a work composed with the hope of eventual publication, accounts for much of its great appeal. In it you see both the candidly recorded vexations of Girl Land and the self-conscious striving to create, on the page at least, a person who would be appealing to others.

When I was young, *The Diary of a Young Girl* was one of the most widely read books in the world. Everyone you knew had read at least parts of it, and most people with at least a high school education had read it in its entirety. But its ubiquity in American cultural life has diminished; it's even possible now to encounter people who have never heard of it. I walked into

a Borders bookstore in Los Angeles a few years ago and asked
one of the clerks—a youngish man, maybe thirty years old—
where I could find a copy of the diary of Anne Frank, and
I was stunned by his answer. Pleasantly, and without a moment's hesitation, he replied, "Who's the author?"

For a moment I thought he was joking, but he wasn't.
I explained to him that Anne Frank was—in every possible
sense—the author of her own life, and he consulted his computer for a moment and then announced happily, "Here it is!
It's in Holocaust!"

He bounded across the store and delivered me to a vast display of books on the subject, and I glanced down, past books
with grim titles and horrifying covers, until I saw her on the
bottommost shelf, smiling out through time in her famous
Montessori school photograph. As the clerk returned cheerfully to his customers and his computer, I realized that Anne's
diary could and did withstand any number of corrosive forces:
the scattering of pages (it was partly composed in a notebook,
partly on sheets of loose-leaf paper) after the war, her father's
editing, accusations that it was a hoax. But the one force it
could not endure, if it was to remain one of the pieces of
writing universally known to young people, was its reinter-
pretation as a work of Holocaust literature. There is not a
single scene set in a concentration camp, and the mention of
roundups and gassing is just that—horrified mention, never
extensive or explicit description. The way the diary was first
read and understood by so many girls for the first years of its
existence would not have been possible had those girls had

the same understanding of the Holocaust that contemporary readers have.

In his book *The Holocaust in American Life,* historian Peter Novick explains that the common understanding of the tragedy as the central moral and historical event of the twentieth century, and as something separate not just from the unprecedented carnage of the Second World War, in which between fifty and sixty million people were killed, but also from Nazi barbarism, is a fairly recent phenomenon. It wasn't until the Eichmann trial of 1961 that the term Holocaust was first used to describe the genocide, and it wasn't until the broadcast of a 1978 four-part television miniseries called *Holocaust*—which had a huge audience, but which was also roundly criticized by, among others, Elie Wiesel, for trivializing and commercializing the event—that the specific nature of the death camps became something about which large numbers of Americans began to have an understanding. All of which, in a sense, is to forgive the way that so many girls read *The Diary of a Young Girl* when it was first published in English in 1952. Yes, they saw her story as tragic, and they all knew from the heartrending afterword that she and the rest of her family except for her father had died in the camps, but they did not read it as a meditation on the horrors of the death camps.

Anne Frank's diary raised the intoxicating notion that a girl's journal might be like that of a great general, or statesman: something that would have a larger readership and importance, something that could engage the interest of others. It might even be something that could make her famous.

Anne Frank understood fame; she was a girl of the modern era. Her diary may have begun as all others do—as a private record of experiences—but it did not stay that way for long. Soon after the family went into hiding, she heard on the radio that the Dutch government planned, once the war was over, to collect letters and diaries for publication, to show what private life had been like during the German occupation. It occurred to her almost immediately that her journal could be just such a document, and the excitement of publication kept her working at it hour after hour—revising pages in loose sheets of foolscap, rearranging material, turning it into a book. This notion of an audience is surely responsible for some of the book's most famous and (to me) least attractive sentences. She writes, "Neither I nor anyone else will be interested in the musings of a thirteen-year-old schoolgirl," a little depth charge of innocent wonder in the middle of the thing. "I still believe people are basically good," she writes in the book's most famous and least convincing declaration. The more winsome Anne—winsome in the sense of being wholly natural and all girl—appears in the less guarded moments. Hers is a book in which every thought is conveyed with an intensity of emotion, a depth of feeling, that is exquisitely pitched to the girl ear. On the one hand she is an imp, a brat, a narcissist, a sulker, a manipulator, a manic talker, a flirt, and a person who insisted on the rapt attention of everyone around her at one moment, and on the pure privacy that all misunderstood people demand at the next.

Anne had proven to girls that it was possible to combine a

set of seemingly contradictory impulses: to live in secret and to become a celebrity; to keep one's innermost thoughts in a private diary and then publish them for all the world to see; and to take the raw material of Girl Land—deeply felt emotion, sensitivity as an end in itself—and to make of them not the basis for a thousand sulks and private poems, but a public and hugely successful manifesto.

We all began to write that way—as though we never expected anything to come of our little musings, but with the secret and fervent hope that our own school pictures would one day be stamped on the cover of our life stories. How close we were to having all the raw materials! Granted, no Nazis. But there, in the wallpapered bedrooms of America, perched earnestly atop our chenille bedspreads, we poured out our hearts—Dear Sharon, Dear Jenny, Dear Kim.

Giving a diary a first name, the way Anne had, conferred on the volumes the attributes of an actual friend. The love that Anne poured out not to her diary, but *for* her diary, was love for a part of herself, and this unbridled, almost cloying kind of pure affection and acceptance is deeply attractive to the girls who read the book. "I'll begin from the moment I got you," begins Anne's second entry, "the moment I saw you lying on the table among my other birthday presents.... A little after seven I went to Daddy and Mama and then to the living room to open my presents, and *you* were the first thing I saw, maybe one of my nicest presents."

As Francine Prose has noted in *Anne Frank: The Book, The Life, The Afterlife:* "What gave the volume its power is that the classic struggles of adolescent female puberty were dramatized against a world crisis and horror of unequaled dimension." The adolescent feeling of being crushed by forces directed exactly at the young soul aspiring only toward beauty and truth was, in Anne's unusual case, actually what was taking place. The American teenyboppers and earth angels who first read the book in 1952 may have lived without the oppression of the Third Reich, but they had all of Anne's other burdens to shoulder: the family drama, in which the mother is newly revealed as an overbearing monster, the sibling who gets the preferential treatment, the physical development that sometimes took an unpleasant or unlovely turn (a certain amount of Anne's time in hiding was devoted to bleaching her little mustache), the feeling of being chronically misunderstood by those who are supposed to love and understand you best.

But what really acted as a sky hook upon the imagination of girls was the notion that their diaries could be at once the places where they shared their innermost thoughts, their dreams and longings, and also a vehicle for becoming famous, the girl hero, the one who transcended all of the cruelty and injustice of her own world and was recognized for her suffering, for her goodness.

What Anne's diary is concerned with more than any other single subject is domestic life, the making of a home, which has proven itself to be one of the most enduring girl subjects of all time: the Laura Ingalls Wilder books, *A Tree Grows in Brooklyn, Mrs. Mike, Little Women*—all of these classics include long descriptions of the routines of housekeeping. The Franks' first day in the secret annex is one of homemaking pure and simple: the place was crammed with boxes of possessions, china and linens they had stored ahead of time, and "if we wanted to sleep in properly made beds that night, we had to get going and straighten up the mess." Margot and her mother flopped down on bare mattresses, absorbing the first shock of what had happened to them, but Anne and her father—"the two cleaner-uppers"—set to work making beds and setting things right. Her father had brought her postcard and movie star collection, and Anne took a "brush and a pot of glue" and "was able to plaster the walls with pictures. It looks much more cheerful." These are the best parts of the book, the least writerly, the most evocative.

Anne in the annex is Francie in the tenement in *A Tree Grows in Brooklyn*, making her own little annex away from the world on the fire escape on a warm Saturday afternoon:

"She put a small rug on the fire-escape and got the pillow from her bed and propped it against the bars. Luckily there was ice in the icebox. She chipped off a small piece and put it in a glass of water. The pink-and-white peppermint wafers bought that morning were arranged in a little bowl, cracked, but of a pretty blue color. She arranged glass, bowl and book on the window sill, and climbed out on the fire-escape. Once out there, she was living in a tree. No one upstairs, downstairs or across the way could see her. But she could look out through the trees and see everything."

Anne, too, had a hundred routines and rituals of making

a home. There were epic, all-hands-on-deck spates of strawberry-jam making (they had been engaged in one such the day before they were routed by the SS), and there were formal meals, and even visitors, who came with library books and fresh produce and all in all it was "really not that bad here."

The other magical feature of the annex was the way the occupants led double lives. On weekdays they had to creep around as silently as possible: every cough had to be stifled with codeine; reading and writing took place, as these were noiseless endeavors; and dinner-table conversations were whispered, as though those in residence were a company of ghosts, assembling for an invisible meal.

But then—nightfall. Like creatures from a fairy tale—like the Borrowers, who had to leave a house if they were ever glimpsed, if even for a moment, by one of the legitimate occupants—they emerged from behind the bookcase door and had the run of the place. They played parlor games, they spent time downstairs in Anne's father's office, "the showpiece of the entire building. Elegant mahogany furniture, a linoleum floor covered with throw rugs, a radio, a fancy lamp, everything first class." Next door to that office, which they could use at night, was "a spacious kitchen with a hot-water heater and two gas burners, and beside that a bathroom. That's the second floor." Some nights, Anne would commandeer the office for her elaborate bedtime toilette, one that included baths and manicures.

The book also concerns another of the main preoccupations of female adolescence, the family romance, that is, the idealization of the father and the constant criticism of the mother. "Daddy's always so nice," Anne writes of her beloved father—her "Pim"—and one of her chief occupations in the annex is finding ways to express her ardor for him. At night, she would crawl into her father's bed for comfort, and when his hair grew too long it was Anne who took over the wifely task of cutting it. With triumph, one day she reports: "I finally told Daddy I love 'him' more than I do Mother." As for poor Mrs. Frank, who does nothing but worry about her daughters, mend their raveling bathrobes, make elaborate and dangerous plans to get Anne new eyeglasses, there is only the disdain and hauteur that is the pubescent girl's special gift to her mom. Anne would like "to give Mother a good shaking," she tells Kitty; she'd like to scream with frustration over being raised by such a rude and useless woman. "I'm beginning to hate her!" she writes at one point, and—typical for her kind—she begins to dismiss all mothers; neither she nor Peter, a teenage boy whose family was also in hiding, really *has* a mother, in her opinion, for both women are so beastly and unhelpful. Mother, writes Anne, "has wounded me thousands of times"—but all she reports on are the minor corrections and small disciplines that all good mothers exert over their growing daughters, hardly the stuff of a great wounding, at least to the nonpubescent girl. Pathetically, at one point her mother accepts the rejection and tells Anne sadly, "I can't make you love me!" which throws Anne back upon herself, and she regrets speaking to her mother so harshly.

Much of what goes on in a young girl's diary is posturing,

and the extent to which Anne actually did express to her mother the feelings she wrote down will remain a mystery, but surely had her mother ever chanced to read that diary, she would have been in for a painful shock.

Although the impulses that attract girls to diary-keeping remain unchanged, the ways that they express and explore those impulses has altered over time, chiefly because of the Internet. In fact it seems to be only the very youngest girls who keep old-fashioned pen-and-paper diaries. American Girl, the purveyor of expensive dolls dressed in period costumes, has a line of advice books for girls. *A Smart Girl's Guide to Sticky Situations,* one of the most popular titles, covers all manner of girl disasters, including a tampon falling out of your backpack ("Pick it up—*quick*") and losing control of your in-line skates ("Head for some *grass*"). But in the section devoted to the most dire situations—those organized under the rubric of "Saving Face"—there is a clear number one, the ultimate sticky situation: what to do if someone reads your diary.

The counsel is wise, involving the strategically brilliant defensive posture of not screaming or crying, for those acts will "let her think she's got the goods on you." The author reminds girls to avoid the problem in the first place by always remembering the importance of an excellent hiding spot, rolling up the secret tome in a pair of old sweatpants, for example, or behind the other books on your bookcase. But most important of all, a girl should never, ever leave her room without safeguarding the diary: "If it isn't in your hands, it should be in its place." Secrecy has always been at the heart of diary-keeping; it is the reason, after all, for all those tiny padlocks and hidden keys.

In 2008 a young woman named Sarah Brown published *Cringe: Teenage Diaries, Journals, Notes, Letters, Poems, and Abandoned Rock Operas,* a collection of the facsimile pages of girls' diaries, with the selections based on the most mortifying passages each contributor could find in her old journals. "We who have grown up with MTV," she wrote, "are accustomed on some level to having our lives recorded and played back for our amusement." Her volume followed the publication of *The Notebook Girls,* the collective diary of a group of very smart and endlessly wisecracking teenage girls. It's composed of entries they wrote to one another while attending the ultra-competitive Stuyvesant High School in New York. The book is meant to be shocking, and boundary-breaking, and it is those things if you're the kind of person who doesn't think a group of college-bound eleventh-grade BFFs ought to be in the position of getting themselves arrested on the streets of Manhattan, or puffing through a Rastafarian amount of pot, or relaxing with "like, 10 shots of vodka." The girls are from the Upper West Side of Manhattan, the daughters of parents who are clearly besotted with their offspring, although not particularly protective of them. The girls disappear into apartment bedrooms with this boy or that one; they are forever being left home alone for long weekends, which inevitably means they end up very drunk or very high and taking care of one another—cleaning vomit out of elevators, for example—

as they go through the throes of experimentation. They have a lot of semi-anonymous sex, some of which they come to regret, and they are concerned to the point of obsession with their college prospects. They seem like little terrors, yet in the girlishness and innocence of their shared enterprise — writing letters to one another, brimming with affection and support — they could be girls from any era of the American past. The way they use the diary to puzzle over the meaning of their sexual experiences is not very different from the nineteenth-century girl who entered a star in her diary for every kiss she got.

The only one of the Notebook Girls who decides to graduate from casual sex to a relationship with a boyfriend writes about their first sexual encounter shyly, in a way devoid of the brazen shock talk of her previous accounts. She tells the other girls what he had said to her afterward: "I'm so glad we did it because I feel so much closer to you." And here it is, even among the fast set of the Upper West Side, in the dawn of the twenty-first century: the old incantation, the one that can turn any grubby high school boy into a modern-day Petruchio, able to tame the wildest girls, if only he will learn its simple words. It's one of the girl's last entries in the group diary, in part because they were on the verge of graduating from high school, but also clearly because now the enterprise has outlived its usefulness: her sexual desires and her emotional ones — for "closeness," for romantic involvement — had at last been aligned, and Girl Land was receding quickly behind her.

·

★ ★ ★

Today's girls have merged the private and public nature of diary-keeping by using the Internet as a place to both reflect on their emotional lives and to broadcast the ephemeral enthusiasms and personas of their Girl Land. For some unfathomable reason, teenagers think that their self-expression on social networking sites is a form of communication between them and the entire global population, except for their parents, their friends' parents, and their teachers. Mothers often feel as conflicted and voyeuristic about checking out a daughter's online revelations as they do about her actual diary entries. In fact, the online life of a girl is usually as much of a construct as a diary—composed of equal parts genuine revelation and practiced put-on.

The primary engine of the stupendous growth of social networking sites like Facebook isn't the Internet itself, but the fathomless narcissism of the young. There's no more ardent devotee of an online profile than its creator, lovingly adjusting the lighting on the perfect self-portrait, changing the song that serenades it, the graphics that surround it. The page can speak broadly to others, but others are almost beside the point; every profile is a sonnet to the self. Today's girls spend hours looking at their profiles, fiddling and tinkering with them—much as I once sat in front of my vanity mirror, holding up my hair and letting it fall, smiling one way and then the other. For girls, the powerful need to be alone in their bedrooms—dreaming, writing in diaries, looking at themselves in the mirror—is married to a kind of exhibitionism. Why was I trying out my hair so many different ways, if not to calculate its potential effect on others? The Internet makes it possible to combine these two opposed desires: to be alone trying something out and to be exposed in public for everyone to see.

Allowing girls to have Internet connections in their bedrooms is one of the worst decisions a parent can make, because it violates the space—physical and psychological—of that room, and it robs them of the essential requirements of keeping a diary. For generations, a girl alone in her room was understood to be doing important work. Away from the influence and pressures of her friends, no longer required to keep up the public persona that school and other activities demanded of her, she could dream, think, read, reflect. The constant refrain that teenage girls hear—from teachers and magazines and parents—is to be "themselves," to feel unafraid to be true to their own ideals and self-constructions, not those of the herd. It was during this time of private reflection, often alone in her room, that a girl felt free to begin to explore that self, and to come to terms with which aspects of her identity would make the transition through Girl Land with her, and which would be left behind forever.

During my junior year of high school, which was the epicenter of my own experience of Girl Land, I owned a a plugugly forest green tracksuit, and I can remember coming home from school every day, stalking into my room, and in one long but fluid series of movements sliding the door shut (for complicated reasons, I had glass patio doors and a curtain instead of a regular door), pulling off my jeans, and stepping into the tracksuit pants. Then I would open the window, let the cat in, and sit on the bed and stare at the wallpaper for an hour. The unattractiveness of the sweatsuit was in part necessary to its total comfort, but also a statement to myself: I was home now, away from everybody, no longer required to look any certain way, or be any certain way. In fact, I was so completely home that I could put on the ugliest thing I owned and still be okay. The people at home—as maddening and shortsighted as they clearly were—would certainly not think any less of me if I showed up wearing it to dinner. I had just spent all day being a teenage girl in a big public high school where the various romantic possibilities, the endless breakups and new attachments of my many friends and rivals, the constant anxiety about whether I would bump into one boy or another in the library, had been a considerable drain on my imaginative life. But back in my room, with the cat and the glass doors and the curtain pulled across them, I could let go.

The Internet has changed all of that. Today's girls leave the hothouse environment of school and peers, retreat to their rooms, and instead of getting a break from the pressure, they reenter it. The dramas of the day continue, the whispering campaigns and gossip need to be constantly monitored, the green sweatsuit or its equivalent can never be donned because the computer has its camera endlessly seeking new images, eager to blast the girl, in her most flattering look, into a zillion screens around the world. Instead of writing her private thoughts in a secret diary, reflecting on herself, becoming herself, alone and in the security of her room, she does so out loud for all to see. She must perform all the time. Is there any wonder that when she finally reemerges for dinner, she's as testy and worn out as she was when she got home from school three hours earlier?

Coming to terms with the new life, emerging as a young woman, becomes ever more intense, because the more a girl realizes how much has changed, the further and further away she gets from the old territory. Meanwhile, the Internet and the various social networking sites to which she is so deeply attracted are ground zero for the contemptuous attitude currently directed at girls and young women. Online, she is asked not just to prolong her exposure to the influence of peers and commerce, but to participate in the creation of a persona that is vulgar, highly sexual, crude. There is no break at all if she retreats to a room with an Internet connection, and so the most essential aspect of diary-keeping is lost to her.

CHAPTER FIVE

Sexual Initiation

FOR MOST OF HISTORY, the final milestone of Girl Land was sexual initiation. Whether the act occurred on a wedding night, and was therefore sanctioned by society and family, as an act of force, or as the consciously made decision of an independent-minded girl, sex was what ruptured your connection to your childhood and changed you forever. But the seventies posed a question that had never before been asked. Was it possible for a girl—living at home, loved, protected from many of the requirements of adulthood—to have the sexual life of a liberated woman, free from the expectation of marriage, and designed purely around her own pleasure? And was it further possible for this to happen within the space of Girl Land, rather than bringing the interlude to an end? Over the course of an agonizing decade or so, the nation's parents worked out a reasonably consistent answer to that question: yes, a girl could indeed have such a life, provided two conditions were met: First, that the number of her partners was small and sequential; and second, that sex took place within a relationship that included romance and courtship, in which sex and love were deeply intertwined. Furthermore, the daughter and her boyfriend needed a comprehensive understanding of birth control and the importance of using it consistently. We take all of this in stride today, but in the late sixties and early seventies, it was the cause of profound cultural foment and anxiety. It was the era of teenage brides and runaways, girls who were desperate to begin their sex lives and also desperately sure that doing so would end their time as daughters in their parents' households.

But with the seventies—the decade that brought women's new sexual freedom to the untested land of girlhood—a new kind of "good daughter" was going to have to be created. This would be the heavy lifting of Girl Land in the 1970s.

Meanwhile, just as the more enlightened mothers were attempting to change their daughters' experience of sexuality, the gathering counterculture was offering new modes of being a teenager, and in particular of being a teenage girl, that were dismaying to the progressive-minded parents and horrifying to the more conservative ones. It was the time of the generation gap, in which young people wanted to kick over the traces of everything having to do with conformity. There emerged three distinct ways for a girl to lead a private sexual life: she could leave her parents (either as a runaway or a teenage bride); she could try to move back and forth between womanhood and cloistered girlhood; or, with her parents' help, she could forge a new path, one that changed Girl Land forever.

1. Runaways and Teenage Brides

If you were a teenage girl in the 1970s you had either read the book *Go Ask Alice,* or seen the television movie of the same title, and probably both. Purporting to be the diary of a typical suburban teenager (and later exposed as a fake), it describes a dreamy, vaguely unhappy sixteen-year-old who falls on hard times when her family moves to a new town where her father, a college professor, takes a job. Lonely, she takes up with a bad crowd, and before you know it she's dropping acid, losing her virginity, getting the family doctor to prescribe her tranquilizers and sleeping pills, and then—with her new supercool best friend, Chris—becoming a drug dealer for two really, really bad college dudes, who end up using both girls sexually and ripping off the money they made selling drugs. So they run away to San Francisco, where, despite some general grooviness (jewelry making, opening their own hip boutique in Berkeley) they end up taking heroin, getting gang-raped, and then—mysteriously—Alice suddenly gets homesick and goes home for a very lovely family Christmas. Everything is turning out great, and Alice's nice boyfriend even drops by the house to renew acquaintances and they share some delicious peanut brittle that her little sister made. On that last page she writes that she's so happy now, and so grown up that she's not going to keep another diary: "Diaries are great when you are young," she writes, but she's older now, and even though the little book has "saved my sanity a hundred, thousand, million times," she no longer has need of it, because now she will be able to discuss her "problems and thoughts with other people." It was the best ending ever, except that when you turned the page, here's what you found:

> The subject of this book died three weeks after her decision to not keep another diary.
>
> Her parents came home from a movie and found her dead. They called the police and the hospital but there was nothing anyone could do.
>
> Was it an accidental overdose? A premeditated overdose? No one knows, and in some ways that question isn't important. What must be of concern is that she died, and that she was only one of thousands of drug deaths that year.

Whoa. The point of the book was to terrify girls, and that's what it did. Drugs, sex, and above all, running away—these were the terrors of the counterculture as understood by millions of middle-class parents, and books like *Go Ask Alice* were intended to terrify us as well.

In the dozen issues of *Seventeen* published in 1969, you can see how this cultural upheaval was making its way even into the staid, conformist world of that magazine, one that often contained ads for engagement rings and silver services, as though the particulars of staging a formal wedding were the most natural thing in the world for a teenage girl to contemplate. But in that year's run of the magazine, the specter of running away from home is mentioned no fewer than twelve times, always with the intention of scaring girls away from it. "If You're Thinking about Running Away from Home" was an article published in February that observed that runaways are looking for "excitement in an atmosphere they think will bring spiritual awakening through communal living—but too often find disaster." The piece included a lengthy interview with a police officer named Tom Rynne, whom the author describes as "no ordinary detective. He is a hippie specialist." Rynne spent much of 1967 and 1968 undercover in Greenwich Village looking for runaways and returning them to their desperate, suburban parents. The head of the New York Missing Persons Bureau remarked on the special appeal that running away held for girls: "The hippies have been played up in the press to the point where the girls feel, for the first time, they are running away *to* something instead of *from* something. They've heard about the gentle, loving flower people and they respond." But the love-in would apparently be short-lived, violent, and—the implication is clear—perhaps involve not just bead-wearing hippie boys, but something far more threatening: black men. "What [runaways] don't know until later, of course, is that behind the façade of sweetness and light are older people waiting to prey on them. Just take a look at Tompkins Square on a Saturday night. It's jammed with cars full of older men—some black, some white—who've come from as far away as the Carolinas. A trusting girl who believes all that talk about free love and communal living can easily end up the victim of a mass sexual assault."

Well, that should have scared the bejesus out of nice girls looking to get stoned in the park and maybe stay out all night, but the responses that met the article in the following month's letter column do not reveal a thoroughly chastened readership. True, a letter arrived from one R.R. in Hialeah, Florida, who wrote, "I wish I'd read it earlier—I ran away at sixteen. I was a child in an adults' world—some people tried to use me." But K.M. from Chicago endorsed running away: "It's an escape, but it's also an awakening. I'll never regret having done it."

There is also a letter from a young woman who is so eager to protect her identity that she has not allowed even her initials or hometown to be revealed. She writes, "I found your article on running away telling it like it is—I spent a month on the Haight before giving it up. I was always a little hungry, and a good deal afraid." This writer's curiously intense level of anonymity, along with her adamantly pro-establishment sentiments, make the letter seem a little fishy. So does her diction, her combination of the expression "telling it like it is" and "a good deal afraid." The former is something a hippie on *Dragnet* might say; the latter, one might expect from a society woman at lunch. Together, they suggest that the mysterious, unsigned missive may have been fabricated closer to the *Seventeen* editorial offices than to the chenille bedspread and tearstained teddy bear of a former runaway.

There was a second form of running away on the minds of girls and parents in that era: running away to get married. Teenage marriage in those years did not mean what it generally means today: a union founded on an unplanned pregnancy. Rather, it offered a way for a girl and boy who wanted to have sex to do so without violating the codes and expectations of the people who raised them. The teenage girl who snuck away to get married incurred her parents' disappointment (and often sacrificed her educational and professional future) but not their disgust: she was having sex and following the rules they had given her.

The September 1969 issue of *Seventeen* carries a piece called "Please Postpone the Wedding." It purports to be a letter from an anonymous father to his seventeen-year-old daughter. He has apparently received a letter from the girl, who is away at boarding school and who hopes to marry her young man shortly after graduation; his letter counsels her against it. Dad proves himself to be a regular Mark Antony in the rhetoric department, beginning his missive by striking an open-minded, soul-of-reason tone: "You may ask how I feel about it. Well, not as instantly and automatically negative as you probably expect. For one thing, I'm pleased that you want my approval, or at least my opinion. For another, I have no ironclad prejudice (I hope!) against teenage marriages. A lot of them fail—one out of two according to the gloomy statistics. But the same number make it, too. We just don't hear much about the good ones." And then, before giving an accounting of teenage marriage so horrifying—the shabbiness of the garage apartment, the chronic shortage of money, the bickering—that I wouldn't be surprised if the girl threw back her boyfriend's fraternity pin in terror and became a lesbian, he enumerates the several advantages of teenage marriage, with a clear number one:

"The biggest plus, without much doubt, is that marriage is the best solution to that most ancient and urgent of social problems: sex. Marriage solves the thorny old dilemma of will-we-or-won't-we, should-we-or-shouldn't-we. Nobody should underestimate this, because sex without fear or guilt is about ten thousand times better than sex that is hung up on broken taboos and lacerated consciences. In our society, matrimony tends to be postponed, for economical or educational reasons, far beyond the time when it makes good biological sense."

Setting aside the yucky issue of a father's instructing his teenage daughter on the secrets of "ten thousand times better" sex, this would have been an excellent moment to introduce the "just have sex with him" advice. But instead it's a knee-clamping litany of debt and quarrels and sleepless, red-faced babies. The daughter is expected not to get married—and also not to have sex. This was the burden for millions of middle-class American girls; their futures were held hostage to their erotic desire in a way that boys' futures weren't. Sophisticated girls from upper-class families tended to have a bit more freedom. Indeed, when Enid Haupt died in 2005, at the age of ninety-nine, her *New York Times* obituary noted that in her distant girlhood, she had made an ill-considered match. Years before her decades-long, happy union with Ira Haupt, the senior partner in a renowned New York brokerage firm, she had run off with a beau in a hasty marriage. She had met him while horseback riding in Chicago and married virtually overnight, divorcing him almost as quickly. It wasn't a shotgun marriage; they never had a child. She had simply done what Anonymous Dad's daughter had wanted to do: ensure that her overwhelming romantic and erotic impulses were safely confined within a marriage. Because institutions such as divorce attorneys and bills of dissolution were not foreign concepts to her parents—because she came from a social class that knew how to redress and obscure the social missteps of its children—the matter was dealt with, quietly, and she was free to do what no middle-class, suburban girl in her shoes could have done: reenter the dating world, relatively unblemished.

Seventeen magazine mediated between the stodgy sexual values of yesteryear and the reality of what life was like for teenagers in America in the wake of the birth control pill, the Summer of Love, and the miniskirt. February's issue carries an essay, "The Feminine Art of Self-Defense," a playlet about two young college kids on a dinner date, which offers coeds a dozen ways to outargue a young man intent on ending the evening in the sack. It was written by the dean of the chapel at Princeton, who proves himself to be a world-class stooge, imagining the scene to be a confrontation between a young man with fire in his loins and a young woman with ice water in her veins. The play proceeds from the assumption that what led so many girls to disgrace was not their erotic desires, but rather their poorly honed rhetorical skills. What hopes did a low-watt girl from a women's college have of debating a Princeton man? It includes the many wily tacks such a suitor might employ, with the coed's earnest rejoinders rebuffing him at every turn. When all else fails—after the sly dog has made appeals to logic, historical precedent, and the time-honored suggestion that she return to his dorm room to take a look at the neat stuff he has up there—he tries a desperate, Hail Mary pass: maybe the girl should go to bed with him simply because she'll enjoy it. Her reply takes the shape of something many girls used to believe: that having sex outside of marriage wouldn't feel especially good.

HE: You say marriage is the best place for sex, so wait until you're married. But some people can't wait. I would have missed a lot of good, clean fun if I believed that. I'm not ashamed of anything I've done. I've enjoyed it. For some people chastity just isn't natural.

SHE: I think two people who wait until marriage are likely to enjoy sex more, have more fun.

Moralists and sensualists may find common ground on the matter of the superiority of marital sex to premarital sex—or then again, they may not. What is at issue here is the great myth that adults used to control the young female libido: that sexual pleasure in women was a force that ripened slowly, perhaps not coming to real fruition until middle age, and that it lasted longer in life than male sexual pleasure. In short, that there was no reason at all to rush, and every reason in the world to wait. It is a notion that fueled adolescent male sex fantasies about teachers and the mothers of their friends—it would make a sensation of the 1971 movie *Summer of '42*—and it was an idea promulgated to girls in order to keep them chaste.

A remarkable article in the July 1969 issue of *Seventeen* reports on a seminar held at Exeter by a physician named Mary Calderone, the sixty-five-year-old educator who headed the Sex Information and Education Council of the United States. Calderone was a sophisticate and a progressive, a daughter of the photographer Edward Steichen. She arrived on campus armed with the kind of information that teenagers across the country were clamoring for, but which most weren't likely to get for several decades. It was the sort of frank and open-minded seminar that could have taken place only at a school like Exeter. The seminar centered on topics that today are routinely discussed in schools: "masturbation, promiscuity, homosexuality, contraception" and also two subjects whose names—and the conditions they conjure—provide an echo of decades past, "sex out of wedlock" and "frigidity." The former, she said, was an abomination, and it was every Exeter man's responsibility to ensure that his sexual needs were not being filled at the risk of bringing an unwanted child into the world. Frigidity was essentially his problem as well: "Sexual response in women is very psychological. If she's angry, if she feels guilty, if she thinks the male is using her as an object or a toy, she may not be able to respond at all." This is sound enough advice, but Calderone presses her point: "By eighteen, a man is apt to experience full sexual response. He reaches a peak of intensity in his late teens or early twenties. From then on the drive begins to lessen, but it never disappears completely. On the other hand a woman's sexual response is much more complex. It comes later, generally has to be learned, and may not reach a peak until the forties. Then it often continues at that level until the seventies."

That a woman's sexual response has to be "learned" is ridiculous. What has to be "learned" is a male's sexual technique. If women start enjoying sex later than men, it's only a reflection of how long it took their same-age partners to figure out what they were doing. The notion of women entering a three-decades-long sexual utopia beginning at the exact year when estrogen begins its steep, irreversible plummet is loony. Women of Calderone's generation were probably relieved to have sex once it no longer carried with it the threat of pregnancy, but saying that the feminine libido gets uncorked at forty is like some hideous joke on *The Golden Girls*. And, for that matter, what accounts for the apparently arbitrary choice of "the seventies" as the end point of a woman's sex drive? Bad knees? Memory lapse? ("Earl, if you know why we're buck naked in the visitors' lounge, you go ahead and tell me.")

The myth of midlife sexual awakening was perpetuated for the same reason the other myths and threats were perpetuated: to keep girls under control. Insisting that they wait until marriage before having sex, or telling them they will regret losing their virginity too soon, or arming them with a thousand ways to say "no," or suggesting that being sexually active would lead to squalor and ruin, to life on the road as a runaway passed among multiple partners ("some black, some white") and—as a last resort for those little hussies who were willing to destroy their reputations for a good time—providing them with inaccurate information about when their sex drives will kick into high gear—all of these techniques were aimed at a single target: repressing the sexual inclinations of young girls, toward the ultimate hope of nullifying them altogether. *Seventeen* magazine presents a world in which boys were crazed with erotic energy and enjoying every chance they had to turn it toward a willing female companion, but in which girls had no equally compelling urges of their own. Of course they did—and that is what makes poignant the advertisements in *Seventeen* for the one kind of goods no contemporary teen magazine ever features: wedding merchandise. The old issues of the magazine are filled with ads for Oneida silver and Lenox china and diamond solitaires. When I look at the ads now, I realize that what was drawing so many teenage girls—girls with college aspirations, and any number of intellectual passions—to short-circuit their futures and become brides wasn't just the allure of orange blossoms and diamond rings, and it wasn't an eagerness to settle down into *Redbook* domesticity as soon as possible. It was, at least in part, their own sexual desire that hastened them forward. It was the same thing that had lured my mother's friends into miserable marriages, and that would betray them just when their study and hard work were about to pay off.

Heartbreaking, too, is the spate of letters that follows each story on sexuality. There is always a letter or two from the kind of girls who agree completely with the wait-till-you're-married philosophy, and who feel an anxious need to parrot it at every opportunity. But there is another kind of letter, one that describes a plight as heartrending to encounter as if it had happened last month instead of so long ago that the letter writers are by now senior citizens. These are letters from girls who, for whatever reason, decided to have sex and lived to regret it. The regrets are never based on the consequences of pregnancy or venereal disease, both of which in the 1960s were such indelible stains on a girl's character that they would have caused her banishment from the letters page of *Seventeen,* as well as from polite conversation. (This was the era when a middle-class teenager who found herself pregnant suddenly disappeared from a community, sent on an extended sojourn to an aunt or a grandmother—or so the neighbors were told—and returning seven or eight months later looking a bit rounder than she had been, a bit hollow-eyed, but otherwise, to the casual observer, no worse the wear for her visit out of state.) The regrets are those of the heart: the boy had turned out not to be the one true love or, worse, he had been a jerk and disappeared after getting what he wanted or—most touching of all—the simple fact that no matter what the relationship with the boyfriend may have come to, the girl no longer feels special, in possession of something of great worth that she alone controls. Sometimes, the girls use the old word: "He ruined me," they will report simply, being not at all histrionic, merely stating a fact. A girl who had lost her virginity was a girl who had been, literally, ruined, like a bolt of silk with a rent straight down the middle. To ruin something, according to the dictionary, is to render it formless, useless, or valueless, which was exactly what many girls felt after giving in to their desires.

2. Patty Hearst: Every Girl

It is within this seventies taxonomy of runaways, teenage brides, and hippie chicks that you have to locate Patty Hearst—for, in a sense, she was a little of each. To understand the reason why her fantastically sui generis story resonated so deeply within so many millions of ordinary American households is to understand that her additional role of kidnap victim has, in the imagination of so many of us, a strong aspect of metaphor. Patty Hearst, of all people, was Every Girl. Regular, ordinary girls were not California publishing heiresses, certainly; nor was the agency of their disappearance abduction at gunpoint. But disappear they did. One moment their lives could be summed up in a series of photographs not so different from the ones flashed on the nightly news over and over again: Patty in a first-communion dress at age eight; smiling with her gaggle of glossy-haired sisters as a young adolescent; sitting quietly—dreamily, inwardly—on the floor beside her mother's chair as a teenager, staring off into the mists of Girl Land. And the next moment—gone.

When I was in grade school, one of my friends had a glamorous older sister who fed the seals at Fairyland—she was long-legged and pretty, and she'd stand in her red miniskirt on a platform, tossing the fish—but then something happened; she went to live down in the flats, and her mother didn't want to see her anymore. There were boyfriends who brazenly took girls out of their houses without chatting up the fathers; there were blue jeans (it is hard to convey the chagrin that middle-class mothers once felt at seeing their daughters in the loathed and stigmatized garment of their own Depression-era childhoods, instead of skirts and ironed dresses and lightweight cardigans). The girls impulsively packed rucksacks and bought Eurail Passes and informed their shocked parents that they were going backpacking in Europe and weren't sure when they'd be coming home. And most of all, underneath it all, there was the line connecting the dots of the Eurail Passes and the screaming matches and even the blue jeans: sex.

Patty Hearst was a rich man's daughter, kidnapped for ransom by a group whose demands were delivered through public "communiqués" sent to radio stations. Clearly she would have made news in any era, but it took something more than the facts of her case, spectacular though they may have been, to account for the impact she had on the American public: between February 1974 and March 1976, she was on the cover of *Newsweek* seven times. The central question about her experience was also being asked in a million tiny dramas that were unfolding across the country—ruptures that turned on blue jeans and broken curfews and birth control pills, rather than on joining a gang of armed revolutionaries: Had this well-tended and much-loved daughter really crossed over? And if she had, was she so far gone that even her own people might not want her back? For several months there, it was *The Searchers* lifted out of Monument Valley and plunked into the filthy coffeehouses and storefronts and communes of Berkeley and San Francisco.

In the beginning of the saga, she was a nice girl, stolen from the safety of her home, who must be rescued with all due speed—before "something" happened to her, that unnamed thing being rape—and then (at the very least) she was a girl who had done whatever it took to survive her captors, who were clearly a revolting bunch. But eventually an awful lot of people became iffy about her. The day after she was caught on the security camera of a Hibernia Bank branch in the Sunset District of San Francisco carrying a semiautomatic carbine during a Symbionese Liberation Army holdup, a nearby homeowner removed the GOD BLESS YOU, PATTY sign in his front yard. When the group was cornered in a house in Los Angeles—one that, in all likelihood, contained Patty as well as her abductors—the police engaged in a firefight that resulted in an explosion that incinerated the occupants, something the cops never would have risked if they had still been thinking of Patty as a victim. Once it was ascertained that she had not died in the inferno and was still on the lam with the two surviving members of the SLA, the DA announced the state's new official attitude toward the young woman who had been dragged, screaming, from her home, one that unintentionally summed up the entire event to perfection: Patty Hearst was no longer to be regarded as the victim of a kidnapping but rather as a suspect in one.

The players in the drama all arrived onstage in the first scene. In Hillsborough, outside a beautiful house with a lacquered black door flanked by topiaries in marble pots, were the missing girl's rich parents, Catherine and Randolph Hearst. She clutched a handkerchief and lifted a hand to the pearls at her throat; he spoke calmly into the microphones, not so removed from his father's empire that he didn't have a newspaperman's instincts for using the press as a means of communicating a single, clear message: demands would be met, the safe return of his daughter was all he required. Patty's prodigious number of sisters, four in all, not one son in the family, also appeared, underscoring the vulnerability of girlhood. They were dead ringers for the lost one, each of them radiating grief and good grooming. In Berkeley was Steven Weed—his improbably perfect surname one of a million fillips to the story—a philosophy graduate student at Cal, slender and pale, sporting a bushy mustache, and badly beaten by the intruders who had burst into the town house he and Patty shared; he came to stand, in the larger narrative, for a certain kind of boyfriend a daughter might bring home in those days, one whose disappointed but savvy parents would be wise to file under the category "Could Have Been Worse." He may have been shaggy and unprepossessing—it was immediately clear that the first time he had been paraded through that lacquered front door in Hillsborough was not a joyous occasion—but he had been living with Patty as her "fiancé" (they had even posed for that most touching of bygone traditions, the engagement photograph), and theirs was a very conventional sort of domestic arrangement. They were like the kind of kids who used to live in "married-student housing": he beavered away at his seminar work, she attended classes and worked at Capwell's department store and did their laundry at the Wash House. The members of the SLA—a group of white, middle-class young people ensorcelled by a black thug named Donald David DeFreeze—had, a few months earlier, announced themselves on the local political scene by actually shooting someone, a feat of ambition and marksmanship that distinguished them from the hundreds of other radical cells festering in the Bay Area at the time. And what a target they had chosen: the hugely popular, young, black superintendent of the mostly black Oakland public school system whose patently benign plan to distribute ID cards to the district's students they perceived as an intolerable act of fascist depersonalization.

During Hearst's trial, there was a great deal of testimony from expert witnesses on the concept of brainwashing, which only serves to point out how limited the research was when it came to understanding what happened to Patty Hearst: most studies had been conducted in a military setting, with subjects who were male, trained for combat, and aware that they were engaged in work that exposed them to grave danger. These men had—at the very least—been provided with a set of guidelines on what they were allowed to reveal to an enemy captor. To place what happened to Patty Hearst into such a context is to allow oneself to be willfully ignorant of the delicate and emotionally charged state of late girlhood, and of the act of passing into young womanhood, a process that for Patty Hearst—because of the sheltering that came with her wealth—was probably slower and more tentative than for many other American girls her age. No one feels sorry for a girl on a yacht, as the saying goes, and much of the harshness that Patty Hearst encountered from the American public, the criminal-justice system, and even many of her own biographers stems from their feelings about the Hearst fortune and history, as though all of those home movies of her grandfather entertaining Charlie Chaplin and Carole Lombard at San Simeon had somehow devolved onto Patty and had made her older and wiser and more experienced than her years suggest. In fact, they had done the opposite.

Patty Hearst was studying peacefully in her bathrobe—she and Steven had eaten the off-campus-housing dinner of champions (sandwiches and Campbell's soup) and had just finished watching *Mission: Impossible* and *The Magician*—when her life exploded into violence. She was beaten, bound, gagged, and thrown into the trunk of a car, and from there she was transferred to a closet, in which she was raped repeatedly and told that she might soon be executed. For the first few days she was not even allowed to use a toilet. During the first seconds of her captivity, she thought she was being buried alive, as Barbara Jane Mackle, the victim of a spectacularly hideous kidnapping, had been five years earlier.

The first sexual assault happened when her hands were briefly freed inside the closet. DeFreeze, whose alias was Cinque, grabbed her crotch and squeezed her breasts, an act that William Graebner, in *Patty's Got a Gun: Patricia Hearst in 1970s America,* characterizes as "fondling" and that a (male) expert witness for the prosecution said was not "sexual assault" but rather an example of Cinque "venting his anger." Can any man understand what it is like for a woman to be sexually brutalized? Patty Hearst was a young woman who had cut short a dream vacation to Europe not only because she missed her boyfriend, but because the behavior of Mediterranean men frightened her: "Rome is really beautiful, but I'm afraid to go out of the hotel alone—men don't just whistle here, they run at you and try to grab you!" She was so moored in the proprieties of her Catholic mother that when she entered an ongoing sexual relationship, she legitimized it (in her own heart, if not her mother's) by placing it within a domestic context, and by sealing its niceness with the promise of a wedding.

And there she was, in the dark, with the first groping eventually leading to the first rape—"he did his thing and left"—

an event made doubly wretched by the fact that she knew the rest of the gang was on the other side of the closet door, listening. Other rapes followed. The SLA was probably the first band of revolutionaries to marry a commitment to radical feminism with the use of systematic rape as a means of recruitment. Terrified in the closet, harangued night and day as part of her "reeducation," dreading the next assault, she discovered that privileges—using the toilet, a chance to brush her teeth with the communal toothbrush—could be earned not by enduring another beating but merely by telling her captors that she agreed with them, that she could see their point of view. Who could hold it against her?

And then she even found a way to stop the rapes, at least some of them. She did it not by resisting the sex, but by falling in love with one of the men who was performing it. In its way, that was a powerful thing to do—to transform the nature of an act by changing the way you think about it. Willie Wolfe was young and good-looking, and not immune to the gratification of having charmed the captive girl whose face was now one of the most famous in the world. They became boyfriend and girlfriend within the SLA—a boyfriend and girlfriend who had to accommodate, within their love, Patty's ongoing role as comfort girl to the other male members and a couple whose relationship included the giving of a special gift: a small, carved monkey on a leather thong that, as Patty tells us girlishly in her memoir, *Every Secret Thing,* was Wolfe's "most treasured possession."

It was a particularly feminine thing to do, to try against all the odds to place one's sex life within the context of romance and affection, and—another irony—it was one of the things that led to her guilty verdict at trial. In her purse at the time of her arrest was the little monkey, the double of one found underneath Wolfe's charred remains in the Los Angeles safe house. Before these charms were introduced into evidence, the jury was on Patty's side: "Everyone's heart went out to her," one juror said of the group's response to the kidnapping, beatings, and rape. "How could you help it? We felt overwhelming sympathy for her." The evidence about the bank robbery was compelling, but that little trinket from the boyfriend hardened everyone's heart. "That was what changed my mind," said one female juror. "I really saw how much she was lying. It just had to be lying, through and through." Love and sex: they will catch a woman up every time.

Patty Hearst, this creature with the glittering past and the famous name, was engaged in a bit of youthful reinvention at complete odds with—and therefore much more original, and even more outrageous, than—that of the city's thousands of other students and young drifters. While they were involved in a self-conscious attempt to shake their middle-class mores and expectations, she was trying, just as self-consciously— Capwell's, the Wash House—to adopt those mores. She was trying to create a life for herself that was not like her mother's but was more in line with the happy lives she saw depicted on television—she was a fantastic television watcher before her capture—and the kidnapping put an ugly and abrupt end to that sweet intention.

Patty Hearst caught our attention because she was an innocent and largely naive young woman who was being fought over, in public, by two powerful forces: her parents and "the culture," in its most extreme and violent manifestation. At one particularly heartrending moment, her father defended her against charges that she had joined the SLA: "We've had her 20 years; they've only had her 60 days," he said. Then Catherine Hearst broke her usual silence: "I know my girl." That's why we couldn't let the story go, not because Patty herself fascinated us, but because we were desperate to know, in the epic battle for her affections, whom she would choose: Catherine or Cinque? It was the kind of question many of us were grappling with in our own lives, and Patty Hearst gave us the perfect excuse to talk about our own situations without really talking about them, not directly. We needed someone like her just then. As the U.S. attorney said in his closing arguments, by way of reminding the jurors how Patty had ended up on trial: "She didn't call us. We called her."

3. Tammy Bellah: In and Out of Girl Land

A few years ago a friend I grew up with in Berkeley called and asked me if I had known Tammy Bellah. She was a Berkeley girl, a decade older than we were, who had killed herself at age nineteen in 1973. The name was familiar and it turned out that she had three younger sisters, one of whom, Abby, had also died young: after a night of partying she and some friends had flipped a car on Marin, which is a very steep street leading from the highest point in the city all the way to the flats. I remembered that incident—the car had come to rest outside of the fence of my elementary school, which had given the event a lurid frisson to us children, and Marin itself was the site of many similar teenage sorrows, giving it a haunted quality. My friend told me that the girls' mother, Melanie Bellah, had published books about both of her lost daughters, and he said that I should read the one about Tammy, that there were certain things I would recognize in it. He was right. The seven-hundred-page doorstop of a book reminded me in many powerful and uncomfortable ways about what Berkeley was like in those days, about the ways in which so many parents had decided—not out of laziness, but out of a combination of certain philosophies and of a youth culture that had outpaced their ability to comprehend or control it—to give their teenagers a tremendous amount of freedom. The city was awash in kids who came from respectable families but who were pursuing lives that no middle-class parent today would ever condone, would in fact horrify them. *Tammy: A Biography of a Young Girl* is like the real-life version of *Go Ask Alice,* about the ways in which it was possible, bit by bit and with your parents right beside you, to slip away into drugs and a kind of masochistic, anonymous sex, and all the while to both celebrate and fear what was happening to you.

Tammy consists of Tammy's diaries, letters, poems, stories, and school essays, as well as a long commentary on these documents written by her mother. The commentary—along with the impetus to publish so many private writings—is intrusive; its main thrust is to explain and exonerate the series of strange and often appalling parenting decisions that played a role in Tammy's tragic fate. The document is long, weird, and compelling. It describes a girl and a family whose lives were strange and extreme, and whose philosophies and inclinations, when combined with some of the cultural ideas that were taking root in places like Berkeley in the late sixties and early seventies, were almost destined to result in disaster. They also reveal, in a grotesque manner, the dangers the counterculture had to offer girls.

"Tammy was feminine in the extreme," writes her mother; "by that I mean that she was maternal, devoted to serving others. She was emotional and obsessed with romance and with trying to re-create the security of early childhood. She was idealistic and unfairly critical of herself for falling short of her own ideals." But she was also "self-deprecating...and ultimately a martyr." The martyrdom was sexual: from a young age, Tammy pursued an erotic life without borders or limitations, a fact that brought her great pleasure, but also profound anguish. As she moved through her teenage years, she came to see herself as tarnished by her experiences, "ruined" by them, and the journals record both her increasing self-loathing and a willingness to enter into masochistic affairs with men. Her sexual impulses made her vulnerable in a way that boys are not; at fourteen she made the fateful mistake of letting her friends know how sexually available she was, and soon enough she heard the devastating news that one of her young men let it be known that he liked her only "when she's lying down." Trying to reverse this impression became impossible, and—even in a place as free-spirited as Berkeley— Tammy was saddled with a reputation that haunted and embarrassed her and that she felt she had to justify. She longed to be sexually independent and adventurous, but had an equally strong desire to be loved and cherished, to have casual sexual encounters develop into full-fledged love affairs. It was a pattern of behavior and expectation that set her up for despair on a titanic level. Although she tried to craft an American girlhood on the mores of Anaïs Nin, whose diaries she read and reread, she also fantasized about getting married very young and setting up housekeeping with her one and only, a young man whom she imagined as stepping out of a romance novel: handsome and strong, eager to protect and provide for her.

Melanie and Robert Bellah had been a brilliant couple at Harvard, where he was an academic on the make and she—a Stanford-educated beauty and freethinker—was devoted to raising their four small daughters, whose physical beauty she took as a point of personal pride. ("We are quite lovely to behold," Tammy wrote of herself and her sisters at one point in the stilted language she often favored.) Melanie was also a woman of considerable intellectual ability, which she sublimated into a kind of intense homemaking that was ultimately unsuccessful: intended to make the family feel supremely cared for, it often left them feeling oppressed and anxious. Dirty hands on a clean door handle, messy friends—these were things Melanie could not abide. Still, she was talented: she spent hours shopping for and preparing excellent meals, and she considered the decorating and cleaning of the house as the most serious of pursuits. She would come to expect the same level of domestic precision and detail from her daughters even as she encouraged them forward into the world, to fulfill her own thwarted ambitions.

In her motherly endeavors, she was attended by a team of notables of the kind only Harvard can assemble. The girls' pediatrician was T. Berry Brazelton, and when an astute teacher made the comment that young Tammy might be a good candidate for psychotherapy, Melanie sought out—at a dinner party—no less a person than Erik Erikson to get his advice on the matter. (Her girl did not need therapy, he advised wisely, drink in hand. The Harvard faculty wife, he knew all too well, is a woman to treat delicately.)

The Bellahs were permissive parents, a phrase that to the contemporary reader sounds like a criticism, but in those days was considered the sign of involvement and thoughtfulness. A permissive parent, in the 1960s, was one who simply realized that a child—like an adult—has a capacity for physical pleasure and a desire for autonomy. Giving him a bit of freedom in these regards (something we all do today, without thinking twice about it) was at the core of the practice. As Benjamin Spock advised mothers in *Baby and Child Care:*

"A small child wants to do a lot of things that get him dirty, and they are good for him, too. He loves to dig in earth and sand and wade in mud puddles, splash in water in the washstand. He wants to roll in the grass, squeeze mud in his hands. When he has chances to do these delightful things, it enriches his spirit, makes him a warmer person, just the way beautiful music or falling in love improves an adult. The small child who is always sternly warned against getting his clothes dirty or making a mess, and who takes it to heart, will be cramped. If he becomes really timid about dirt, it will make him too cautious in other ways, too. It will keep him from developing into the free, warm, life-loving person he was meant to be."

It was, in its way, a radical bit of advice, in keeping with a whole philosophy that would be a recipe for many happy childhoods and an entire generation of unhappy and often disastrous adolescences. Letting a toddler do whatever he wants, under the watchful eye of a mother, is entirely different from letting a teenager, away from home for long hours and tempted by any number of new and potentially malevolent forces, do whatever he wants.

In the Bellahs' spacious rented house in Cambridge, the children were encouraged to let their imaginations soar. It was Girl Land complete: endless games of Fairyland and Queen of the May and Cinderella. Melanie's intense interest in her daughters' early girlhood found expression in a hundred ways. She seemed to wish they would stay little forever. Their early babblings delighted her so that she wrote a storybook called *Baby's First Sounds,* which was published as a Little Golden Book. There was heart-shaped cinnamon toast for breakfast every Valentine's Day, matching black velvet dresses every Christmas, excursions to the ballet. Each time a new baby came along, Melanie fixed up another room in the house so that each girl could have her own enchanted principality. Both parents were determined to make the family the center of each little girl's emotional universe, and they encouraged a kind of mythmaking about themselves, almost a private language about who they were: the two younger girls were nicknamed the Liddlies; the two older, the Biggies; Melanie was a kind of Marmee March, subject of poems and love letters and reveries of adoration and devotion. Melanie's housekeeping was a point of absolute pride, and its intention was to provide the family with a home of complete comfort and delight, a place that far exceeded anything the rough outside world could ever offer. As in a fairy tale the girls were tiny and exquisite, like their mother; even in adulthood, some would never reach ninety pounds. The girls spoke to and about one another in the fluttery, nineteenth-century language of girl love. They all kept diaries and they all wrote secret letters to one another in which they spoke to "my darlingest," "my own sweetest," "my own special, beautiful girl." Melanie addressed the girls in similar fashion, and she referred to Robert by a series of nicknames, including Daddy, and sometimes Tado, which he maintained was the name that his childhood cat addressed him by. There was something pressured and cloying about all of this, a sense that the girls could never grow up, because what would Melanie do then?

By sixth grade, Tammy was having schoolgirl crushes of consuming intensity. First there was Vance. "Oh Diary! There is a boy in school. His name is Vance, and I like him. He is nice." Then Rick, whom she walked home with and adored, but who made "gross comments to her." Yet she endured them: "No matter how mad I get, I'll always love him, awfully." Then Jack, and on it went.

But before any of these romances could take flight, there was big news, delivered, on the cusp of her thirteenth birthday: Robert had been offered a position at Berkeley, and he planned to take it. "C'est la fin de ma vie en Cambridge," Tammy wrote, and in short order Melanie had packed up the whole kit and moved the Bellah family base of operations. They bought and restored a house that only permissive parents would deem a good choice for a family containing four very young, impressionable, and pretty girls. It was divided into two separate residences: the upstairs contained the kitchen, living and dining rooms, and master bedroom; and the downstairs (connected to the main rooms by an exterior staircase, and entered through a door leading outside) was an apartment of rooms where the children lived. This was not to be a happy arrangement for Tammy, who needed far more supervision than her permissive parents were inclined to give her.

In California, Tammy's schoolgirl interest in boys took off like a rocket: she began sleeping with them at the age of fourteen. At that point she asked her mother for birth control pills, and Melanie fretted that she was too young for sex— worried, explicitly, in fact, that if she started so early other girls would "gossip" and Tammy would get a "reputation." But Tammy whispered that she was "weak": she feared she could not contain her own sexual passion.

These words would have fallen differently on the ears of a mother not dedicated to permissive parenting. The idea that such a young girl was so threatened by the force of her own sexuality that she saw it as a "weakness," a word that speaks volumes about how she was feeling toward this emerging impulse, might have caused other mothers to investigate the situation, impose limits, talk to their girls. But just as Melanie had allowed her girls to play in water and dirt when they were little—for the simple pleasure of it—and later allowed them to use heroin (again, because the girls thought it was fun), she thought of Tammy's decision to become sexual as something she should not thwart but rather encourage.

Tammy's course was set at the age of fourteen, when she began having sex and also speaking openly about the fact to her friends, and it was then that she discovered one of the harsh and enduring truths about young female sexuality: if a boy has a lot of sex at a young age he is a person to be admired, but if a girl does she is subject to the most painful kind of ridicule. Tammy quickly developed a reputation as being not just "easy" but the "whore of Berkeley," and this fact caused her to suffer. Yet at times she tried to embrace the idea, as though it had been her own. In a few short years, however, her sex life became a tool of her own self-loathing, the instrument of her degradation. By fifteen she had attempted suicide; by the age of seventeen she had a lover who beat her; by eighteen she was begging men to slap her; and at nineteen she locked a bedroom door against the ex-con junkie she had been sleeping with and killed herself. The bed she died in was her mother's, and that is the most poignant element of the baleful story: Tammy kept trying to go home, to crawl back through time, not just to the days before she was known as the girl anyone could have sex with if he wanted, but to the time when she was a little girl, a creature who could crawl into her parents' bed and take a nap, wake up and be safe, recovered, her old self again.

It would later turn out that her sexual initiation had begun when a boy had "semi-raped" her, but when she made this alarming confession to her parents, they did not react to the news with much rancor toward the boy, who was already off the scene, and Tammy began sleeping with other boys at an astonishing clip. Their names seem to change with every page: Gary, Daniel, Jeff, Arthur. She wrote openly about the experiences. "We made out on his bed and Ben made it to third base and it was pure ecstasy, my face red and sweating, when he stopped," but then "we made love and it hurt (it still hurts)," she wrote piteously, "but I did not cry out once." Her true desire, we sense quickly, wasn't exactly—or certainly not only—sexual. "Ben, arms holding, hearts beating, sweat streaming love." She wanted desparately to love and be loved.

She attended an alternative high school and began an abusive and sexually humiliating relationship with a thirty-five-year-old black man who she said made her feel deeply ashamed of being white, and who manhandled her, leaving bruises on her arms. "He is intensely critical, cannot tolerate weakness of any kind, and is extremely authoritarian." Still, "I crave sex with him and always want more."

"Love and sex are what is most important to me," she wrote in a manifesto of her youth, but usually what she got was the latter, and often accompanied not by love but by degradation. Over and over again, she assumed that the sex would produce a certain level of commitment, even of friendship, in the boy or man she was currently sleeping with, and time and again she was proven wrong. At seventeen she began dating a thirty-year-old Green Beret ("he gets hard at the drop of a hat"), whom her parents did not care for, and by eighteen she had been accepted to Berkeley.

Just before Tammy's freshman year of college, her parents and sisters moved to Princeton for a sabbatical year, and she fell apart. She missed "Mommy and Daddy," she wanted her mother to send her the recipes for special meals—beef Stroganoff, coffee cake, waffles—and to pay for a new electric beater so she could try some more adventurous things. But her mother didn't want her cooking in the kitchen, wanted her to use the on-campus dining plan she had paid for, and Tammy—already a heroin user, and someone who had experimented with all the big drugs that were washing through town at that point—began to despair.

"I want to be a little girl again," she wrote repeatedly. "Am I still a girl? Am I a woman? No-no," she wrote. "I am in between." But by that point she was already frequenting the free clinic for VD treatments and pregnancy tests. She became lost in reveries of her past, in writing long, girlish poetry, and in talking shyly about her hopes of a wedding of her own one day. But then she would turn the page of her journal and describe her life with the addict who gave her "orgasms— one or two times" each night, and "never before in the life of Tammy Bellah has this happened!" Here is Tammy grieving the distant shores of her Girl Land, not long before she administered the final, fatal dose of poison:

> The world is sometimes
> a cruel place
> and I want to be
> a little girl again
> And run away.

4. Katherine Danziger: Sex Comes to Girl Land to Stay

When I was a teenager, in the late 1970s, my mother took me aside several times to give me a specific piece of information about sex. I knew that there were mothers and teenage daughters who regularly enjoyed honest, unembarrassed discussions about sexuality, usually while sitting together on a window seat while a slight breeze stirred a pair of gauzy white curtains and a generation-bridging folk song played quietly in the background. We were not such a mother and daughter. If my mother had taken me aside to pull out one of my molars with a pair of pliers, I could not have greeted these episodes with more hostility and undisguised horror.

She knew she wouldn't have much time to talk before I escaped from the room, banging the door behind me, so she picked her moments carefully. She would creep up behind me while I was washing the dog in the laundry room sink, or pouring a stream of colored beads into a lead mold to make a stained-glass window ornament, and then she would suddenly appear, talking the moment she was in range, which was close to my ear because (unstated, but clear) this was not the sort of discussion my father was to overhear.

"Never marry a man because you want to sleep with him," she would begin, talking in the grave and urgent tones you would use to impart the directions for diffusing a bomb. "Just *sleep with him!*" This was the way the talk always began, and I never got all of the subsequent details entirely right because I would have begun my retreat—the wet dog bounding through the back door, the colored beads rolling to the edge of the table. The rest of the lecture had something to do with several girls she had known in nursing school who thought they had to get married before having sex, and subsequently ended up in miserable, loveless marriages.

What I realize now, thirty years later, is that she was giving me permission to have sex if I wanted to, but her frame of reference was so foreign to my experience that I hardly understood what she meant. I was weighing a lot of factors when I thought about losing my virginity, but marriage wasn't one of them. What did she think I was going to do, show up at breakfast one Sunday morning in my blue terry-cloth bathrobe, pour Sugar Puffs into my bowl, and announce that I was henceforth to be addressed as Mrs. Jonathan Krewer?

This was how it was, during that endless, unhappy adolescence: my mother desperately trying to warn me of all of the pitfalls, heartbreaks, and dangers of womanhood but being too ambivalent about her mission to attempt it in a rational manner. We lacked a common vocabulary—of experience, beliefs—in which to have the discussion and so it would inevitably end in my freaking out; and then the two of us working to turn back the clock, to bind ourselves back together as little girl and mother. She would cook me up a special treat or plan an excursion or let me pick out new wallpaper for my bedroom. For my own part, each stir-fry and trip to the Concord Mall for nightgowns or sandals felt like a betrayal of the worst sort, because in those days I really was thinking a lot about initiating a sexual life (as my mother suspected), which made taking her gifts seem like an act of deceit. Could I have the secrecy, adulthood, and risk of sex and also the pink dotted-Swiss dressing gowns and special blueberry pancake breakfasts of girlhood?

I could. That's what she was trying, so unsuccessfully, to tell me. She wanted me to know that she would still love me, and still be my mom, even after I started having sex. A new time had come in the history of American girlhood, and it was based on a complex and perhaps untenable premise: that human sexuality is not a profound and life-altering force that separates childhood from adulthood; that it might be possible now to be two things: a daughter living at home, studying for algebra quizzes and putting Gee, Your Hair Smells Terrific shampoo on my mother's grocery list, and also a young woman beginning a private and womanly sex life. The dream was that a girl could be cosseted and cherished at home, with a carefully decorated bedroom and heart-to-heart talks with her mother, yet at the same time become a sexual creature.

The mothers of the sixties and seventies had been adolescents and young women during a complicated time, the era of the Second World War, an experience that left many of them with a desire to give their daughters something different: more open-mindedness in matters of sexuality. Although many of these women became housewives and mothers, broadcasting to the world and to one another the social conformity that was the hallmark of the postwar years, their experience of being young during wartime had been more nuanced than was generally assumed. As Gay Talese writes of this generation in *Thy Neighbor's Wife*, a large number of young women had in fact initiated their sexual lives when their boyfriends or fiancés were deployed overseas, something they kept closely guarded: "It would have been almost unpatriotic not to regularly write V-mail expressing encouragement and hope and loving lies, suggesting a sexual fidelity at home that was often as fictional as that of their lovers overseas.... While they wrote letters to men they loved, they made love to men they didn't, and along with this varied experience and experimenting they developed a tolerance and understanding that would one day contribute to their permissiveness as parents, a permissiveness that would be condemned by the moral critics of the sixties." Until the sexual revolution and the Pill pushed their way into Girl Land, it seemed possible for parents to allow well-protected daughters an adolescence that included sexual interactions with boys that fell short of intercourse; since the twenties, the idea of petting—an activity that by definition fell short of inter-course—had been a part of the experience of millions of middle-class teenagers. Widespread teenage sexual inter-course was held in check by fear of pregnancy, and by the enormous societal stigma about being an unwed mother; girls' fathers kept callow boys in line not by writing snappy self-help books about their daughters' ruination. Rather, the young men would end up married or run out of town, at the very least.

As a teenage girl in the early 1970s who was desperately cu-rious about sex, I read everything I could lay my hands on. I turned to novels for information not just because I'm a reader but because when I was young they were among the few places a nice girl could find any. (*Love American Style* was risqué, but it was hardly explicit.) To my parents' dismay I read *Valley of the Dolls* more times than I could count, but Jacqueline Susann's attitude toward human sexuality was on a par with her prose: whorish and dirty. *Goodbye, Columbus* commanded my attention, but you don't turn to Philip Roth if you want to learn how to go all the way with a really nice boyfriend.

Adults were quick to stick you with *The Bell Jar,* which you were supposed to lap up with zesty gratitude because of its racy subject matter, but I smelled a rat from the get-go. Even at sixteen I could tell that the book was overpraised, a stealth weapon of grown-ups eager to appear progressive in their literary suggestions for teenagers but secretly dying for you to get an eyeful of Esther's first sexual experience: recovering from a suicide attempt, on furlough from a psychiatric ward, she does the deed with an older man and almost hemorrhages to death.

The only books I'd seen that placed sex where I wanted to find it—in the middle of a committed relationship, with the boy treating the girl as if she were the most important person on earth, and their love so powerful that it threatened to blot them both out—were the pregnancy-scare books that had been passed from hand to hand among the girls at my Catholic junior high. Written in the 1960s, they invariably involved a supersmart girl (family: respectable, middle-class) and a really neat, ambitious boy (his people would be working-class; their great dream would be for their son to become a college boy). Always the pair would make a terrible mistake one night; always it would be one shot with a bullet: dead rabbit and hell to pay. They would grapple with the most serious kinds of decision-making, and always (this is why we devoured these books and dreamed about them) the couples ended up married at sixteen, living in garage apartments or guesthouses. Books like *Too Bad About the Haines Girl* and *Mr. and Mrs. Bo Jo Jones* were supposed to frighten us away from sex, lest we become tragic girls ourselves. But they were so clearly built upon a commonly accepted and deeply stirring code of male honor—an almost chivalric set of principles, handed down through the centuries and still in practice in the American suburbs of the 1960s—that we were dazzled by them and regarded them as the greatest love stories ever told. Which, in a sense, they were.

And then: Judy Blume's *Forever*. If Hollywood movies of the 1930s taught my parents how to kiss, *Forever*, published in 1975, taught me and my generation how to have sex. This was sex the way girls wanted to read about it, the way they wanted to experience it: immersed in romance. The main character is named Katherine Danziger, but she is really Margaret from *Are You There God?* a few years later, still living in suburban New Jersey, still a good girl with good parents. *Forever* is the first mainstream novel written for American teenage girls that is not only sexually explicit but also intentionally erotic, and that gives them the exact information—practical as well as emotional—to initiate a satisfying sex life.

Katherine and Michael are college-bound high school seniors from nice families. Katherine's parents are so exquisitely in tune with the physical and emotional progress of her relationship that one wonders if they've planted a wire on her. The grandmother who in *Are You There God? It's Me, Margaret* sent sweaters with labels that read "Made Expressly for You…by Grandma" now sends Planned Parenthood brochures with a note reading, "I don't judge, I just advise." Katherine's mother leaves a *New York Times* article about teen sex on her daughter's pillow one night, and they rap about it the next morning. "A person shouldn't ever feel pushed into sex," Katherine tells her mom. "Or that she has to do it to please someone else." Mom says approvingly, "I'm glad you feel that way." Was Mom, Katherine asks, a virgin when she got married? No, but she's had sex only with Dad, and she waited until they were engaged.

Where *Margaret* offered highly specific information about sanitary pads and belts, *Forever* takes us straight to the birth-control clinic, and it doesn't flinch. ("Then he slipped this cold thing into my vagina and explained, 'This is a vaginal speculum. It holds the walls of the vagina open so that the inside is easily seen. Would you like to see your cervix?'") .

Armed with birth control pills, with a code of sexual ethics that center on a girl's cautious willingness and a boy's patient and full commitment to her, and with a final health clearance (Michael admits that the previous summer he contracted VD from his only other sexual partner, but he's fine now), Katherine and Michael are off to the races. Anyone who rereads *Forever* and expects to find it much tamer than she remembers is in for a shock: "This time Michael made it last much, much longer and I got so carried away I grabbed his backside with both hands, trying to push him deeper and deeper into me— and I spread my legs as far apart as I could—and I raised my hips off the bed—and I moved with him, again and again and again—and at last, I came."

It took librarians and parents a decade to decide that *Forever* was pornographic, and it has always been on the short list of banned books, but what was so revolutionary about it weren't the explicit descriptions of sex. It was that at the end of the book, the main character tires of her boyfriend, breaks up with him—to her parents' relief, not because of the sex, but because of his social class; they had always hoped it was a fling—and at the end of the novel, she is happily packing for college and reestablishing communications with an old beau from the top drawer, with the implication that soon enough the two of them will be back to the labors of female orgasm.

The idea posed in *Forever* was that a girl and her parents could reconcile the two forces: the desire for her to be a product of the home, tended and watched over and still the responsibility of her parents, and also that she could have a sexual life, with all of its mysteries, delights, and dangers. For many of today's parents, those who grew up in the time of *Forever* and its arcadia of homeward-leaning but sexually liberated teenage daughters, that has been the goal in raising their own girls. But the culture, as always, presses forward, and the dream has become more fraught with ugliness and threat than Judy Blume's radical but sunny novel suggests.

CHAPTER SIX

Proms

Pᴿᴼᴹ ᴛᴏᴅᴀʏ ɪꜱ ᴀ three-billion-dollar business and the genesis
of more hysterical episodes—between embattled kids and
parents, parents and school administrators, kids and one another—than almost every other aspect of high school life
combined. As anyone remotely connected to prom—the loss
of the definite article seeming to signify its massive position
in the American consciousness, its sui generis nature; it's not
"the prom" just as it's not "the God"—understands, the event
has moved beyond a dance, beyond a night of sexual initiation, into some kind of bacchanalia that defies most adults'
abilities to understand it. As a cultural form, proms encapsu-
late the emotional state of Girl Land. On the one hand they

speak to the romantic yearnings of girls, a force that has certainly been shaped and made more elaborate by commerce
and culture, but which is nonetheless authentic. Proms, like
contemporary white weddings, are schmaltzy and corny, and
they are larded with ritual and symbol, which are by now almost meaningless. They celebrate a kind of sublimated and
deeply safe sexuality, one in which there are chaperones
around every corner. From the birth of prom in the 1930s,
adult authority figures have been delighted to encourage and
nurture its development. Proms stood as a reactionary corrective to the licentiousness of the twenties and reintroduced
adult sanction and supervision to teenage romance. Girls today—just like girls in the twenties—still want to embrace
the now, and they are still budding sexual creatures. Yet they
are forced—perhaps more now than at any other time—to
experience sexuality on boys' terms. The bacchanalian after-
parties that have become as important as the proms themselves are ones in which the manufactured romance of the
school-sponsored event is replaced by a frenzied attempt to
embrace the most coarse and vulgar aspect of the common
culture, in which girls change from prom wear into sleazy
clothes and drink to the point of passing out, both of which
seem to be inclinations supported wholeheartedly by the
boys. So this, today, is the whole equation of prom: the girls
using the formal dance (as they always have) as a public recognition of their enduring attraction to things like corsages and
special dresses and elaborate hairdos, and the boys and girls
together using the after-parties to embrace the culture in

which they are actually growing up. There has always been something bittersweet and emotionally overwrought about proms, and the reason for this centers on the role they play in a girl's departure from Girl Land.

The night before I ended my first marriage, when I was alone in the apartment, I walked to the table in the front hallway and very purposefully set down on it each one of my credit cards, listening for the slight snap of the plastic hitting the polished wood. Then I added my checkbook and a note explaining how much I had taken out of the joint account to get me started in life on my own. I felt sure of myself as I did these things. In the first place, the money in the marriage had been his, and I didn't want him to think there was going to be a fight over it, or that my actions had anything to do with finances. That small gesture constituted one of the only moments during the unhappy and dislocating experience of getting divorced in which I seemed to know exactly what to do, seemed to have been given a script beforehand, as indeed I had been: it was the script from the long opening scene of *Kramer vs. Kramer,* which I had seen as a young woman in college and which had affected me deeply. It might not seem the most appropriate source material for my own drama: my ex-husband and I had no children, and a child custody fight is the premise of *Kramer vs. Kramer.* But I remember being taken by the first scene of the movie, in particular by the nervousness and agitation with which Meryl Streep confronted the bridge she was burning, the way she filled up her suitcases and put her credit cards and laundry slips on the table and then sat on the couch waiting for her husband to come home so she could announce her decision. It seemed an act of great courage and style, and something ticked over in my mind: "If I ever get divorced, that's what I should do."

It's funny the impact that movies—sometimes great ones, just as often corny ones seen at a particular, formative moment—can have on our imaginations, and even on the way we conduct ourselves in private moments, the way we do things like dress and kiss, decorate our bedrooms and set a table for dinner. Movies don't just reflect back to their audiences a way of living, they also help to create one, the two forces supporting each other in countless large and small ways, often resulting in a set of dreams and inclinations on the part of the audiences that the filmmakers could never have imagined. Brian De Palma, for example, cannot have intended his horror movie *Carrie,* in which a prom queen is doused in pig's blood and responds by burning her classmates to death, to be the vehicle by which millions of American girls helped to revive the tradition of prom, which when the movie opened in 1976 was experiencing the same doldrums as were a lot of the old rah-rah customs of high school life. But *Carrie* stirred something in me, as it did in many of my cohorts. The movie wasn't my first exposure to the idea of a prom, but it was certainly my first experience to the specifics of one, the way it could shape an entire senior year of high school. The dresses, the emotionally laden invitations, the way a space as hard-surfaced and unlovely as a high school gymnasium could be transformed into a dream time of romance and teenage ardor. When Carrie and her date stepped into the prom and the camera lovingly drifts over the glittery stars hanging from the ceiling, I sat up in my seat: this was something worth learning more about. I can hardly recall the theme of my own prom, but I'll never forget Carrie's: "Love Among the Stars." With the tuxedoed band and the tables draped in linen cloths, it seemed as though I was being not just informed about something, but reminded of something. The adult sensibility behind the movie *Carrie* is well aware of the kitsch of prom. But the teenage sensibility that young people brought to it saw the prom the way Carrie did—as something almost literally magical.

Today, proms are often called rites of passage, and usually regarded as an actual "right"—something teenagers are owed, something no one can take away from them, like graduation itself. Probing proms for their significance to the kids who attend them and to the parents who pay for them has become a regular subject of cultural and journalistic inquiry. In *Slate,* Ann Hulbert described the distaste that many urbane, sophisticated teenagers had for prom in the aftermath of the sixties: "In the early 1970s," she wrote, "at my unconventional private school in Brooklyn, a prom was unthinkable—a bourgeois and sexist ritual of the traditionalist '50s that our parents might have enjoyed but we, long-haired and liberated, disdained." By the nineties, they had a very different meaning, as Thomas Hine points out in *The Rise and Fall of the American Teenager.* He describes a notorious 1988 episode in which a New Jersey prom-goer, whom no one knew was pregnant, excused herself from her date, went into the women's bathroom, and delivered a baby, which she then smothered in a plastic bag and crammed into a trash can. She promptly returned to her partner and danced the night away, without telling anyone what she had done. As Hine observes:

"By giving birth at the prom, the young woman violated the old-fashioned meaning of prom as a celebration of the end of a protected, almost childish mode of existence. But her act also undermined the more recent tendency by young people to use the event as an aggressive assertion of maturity. She proved herself physically capable of bearing a child, but not mentally, emotionally, or morally mature enough to handle it."

The most common interpretation of proms is that they are a dry run for the big prom of the future. Karal Ann Marling, the author of *Debutante: Rites and Regalia of American Debdom* (2004), devotes a chapter to proms, in which she observes that "today, teenagers with credit cards, cars of their own and a taste for the good life have made the prom into a pinnacle social event, a dress rehearsal for the mega wedding, which has also reached surreal heights of elaboration."

With their limousines, flowers, and apparently limitless propensity for supersizing, proms do have a lot in common with the contemporary white wedding. But, historically, the influence of one event on the other was probably in a reverse direction: proms were born decades before middle-class American girls had any designs on throwing themselves a version of the society weddings they saw in the movies and read about in magazines. If anything, the proms of America, in which middle-class high school girls were free to create for themselves a perfect night of romance and glamour, exerted an influence over the dreams they would go on to have about their own weddings. If there is a jejune quality to many contemporary weddings, it is because the form bears the echo of the dreams of sixteen-year-old girls.

It's hard to believe that something as extravagant and unnecessary as a high school prom would have been born during the Great Depression, but that's what happened.

In a collection of children's letters to Eleanor Roosevelt, *Dear Mrs. Roosevelt,* edited by Robert Cohen, there are heartrending appeals from the young writers for decent clothes to wear. "Dear Mrs. Roosevelt," wrote a fourteen-year-old girl on March 24, 1934, "Will you please send me some clothes, or some money for some if you can?" On December 24 of that year, a teenager living on an Alabama farm wrote, "Mrs. Roosevelt, if you please will send us a few dollars not to pay our debts. But to get us a few clothes to wear."

This is the Depression we are used to reading about, the one in which, in FDR's memorable formulation, a third of the nation was "ill clothed, ill housed, ill fed." A quarter of American wage earners were out of work, a statistic that revealed itself in these desperate attempts to create a wardrobe for a hungry family. At the other end of the spectrum was café society, heavily covered in the media, and the Hollywood fantasy machine, which was turning out movies like *Bringing Up*

Baby and *Top Hat,* showing a glittery world of New York night-clubs and Connecticut country houses. But in between these two poles of desperation and excess was the majority of the country's families, people who had taken an economic hit, but who were not broken, and in the midst of this—in part despite the Depression and in part because of it—the American high school became the cultural institution that it is to this day.

In the 1930s the government had a particular incentive to get as many teenagers as possible enrolled in school: every time it transformed a worker into a full-time student it adjusted the national unemployment figures and took pressure off the job market. During the first two years of Franklin Roosevelt's first term, 1.5 teenagers lost their jobs for this reason. As Hine notes, "Nearly all these job losses were caused by the National Recovery Administration.... Companies taking part in the program were forbidden to employ anyone under eighteen." The prospect of all of these newly idle adolescents, however, came with a new, equally worrisome set of concerns: "Adults seem always to be at least a little frightened by the young," he writes. "During the 1930s, those who looked beyond our borders had reason to worry. Young people had played a strong role in the fascist movement that had brought Benito Mussolini to power in Italy. The Hitler Youth Movement, which looked from this side of the Atlantic like the Boy Scouts from Hell, was 5.4 million strong by the end of 1936.... Throughout the 1930s politicians and commentators across the ideological spectrum warned of the possibility of a demagogue who could mobilize the energies of American youth."

Indeed, there emerged such a demagogue, although a benign one. The American school movement, which began in 1910 and which sought to make free secondary education available to all American teenagers, reached its zenith in the thirties. With it, the jingoistic, galvanizing culture of spirit rallies and sports rivalries and color days marshaled youthful energies. It was the genesis of the American high school experience we know today. WPA crews built or extensively refurbished hundreds of schools and are in part responsible for the iconic look of the American high school, with its poured concrete edifice, streamlined, art deco design, and—always—large auditorium, where students gather for assemblies, plays, rallies. The goal of high school in those years was different from that of secondary education in other Western countries; its purpose was to prepare students for life, not for college. There was often a college track, but there was also a commercial track and a general track, and for most students, high school graduation would mark the end of their formal education. The students in these schools represent a particular and often historically neglected demographic of the Depression years. The high school movement, begun in New England, took hold most forcefully in places where there was a large, stable, and typically homogeneous population of middle-class families, people whose incomes might have been reduced—sometimes severely so—by the economic crisis, but who were financially solvent and thus able to provide for an able-bodied adolescent's pursuit of something as economically unproductive as high school. They headed off in the morning in yellow school buses (the thirties saw the standardization of these vehicles), or packed into cars, and they returned, not overburdened by homework but engaged by complex, civically minded, and often explicitly patriotic social and extracurricular programs.

Amid all of this, the prom was born, fully formed, and in many significant regards it is unchanged all of these long years later. Eric Hobsbawm, editor of *The Invention of Tradition,* defines an invented tradition as one in which a certain ritual is created out of whole cloth with a specific intention: not to represent any particular fact or status but to "make it seem to have emanated, directly, and without interruption from the historical past." An example he gives is the pageantry that surrounds the British royal family in its ceremonial functions, all of which seem to have come from the "immemorial past" but which are in fact products of the late nineteenth and early twentieth centuries. Hobsbawm identifies two varieties of invented tradition: one that is "actually invented, constructed and formally instituted, and those emerging in a less easily traceable manner within a brief and dateable period—a matter of a few years, perhaps—and establishing themselves with great rapidity." It is in this second category that proms belong; you can't find a single mention of them in American high school yearbooks of the 1920s, but by the mid-1930s they were cropping up all over. Even the name is a bit of invention. It may be a nod to the English tradition of the last night of proms, when young people dressed up to attend the final in a series of concerts held at the Royal Albert Hall, and it may have been a gesture toward the grand march that some proms had, when couples promenaded, straight-faced, around their high school gyms, dressed to the nines and observed solemnly by their chaperones and by the younger classmates who helped to throw the event. But the word was probably chosen for its obvious, drop-dead fanciness, the type imagined by teenage girls. Fanciness has always been one of the most important elements of proms.

Crumbling in my hands, its publication date 1938 and its original price seventy-five cents, *The Junior-Senior Prom: Complete Practical Suggestions for Staging the Junior-Senior Prom* is widely agreed to be the first piece of published material on the subject. It was written by the team of Marietta Abell and Agnes J. Anderson, who produced a series of similar books throughout the decade, distributed by an outfit in Minneapolis called the Northwestern Press, which identified itself as "Publishers and Distributors of Entertainment Material." The two women also wrote *Programs for High School Assemblies, Drama Clubs in Action,* and *Pep Meeting Stunts;* collectively these books give us proof of the importance in the thirties of creating a national culture within the American high school.

The Junior-Senior Prom is a strange book because of its paradoxical dual purpose: on the one hand it must instruct readers on exactly how to throw a prom, but on the other it must do so as though the reader already knows everything about proms, and indeed has gone to one herself. The book is directed not at teenagers, but at the teacher who has been given the task of sponsoring the prom and "who teaches a full schedule of classes and who must work with her committees during after-school hours." It offers specific directions on how to hold an event the likes of which they have probably never seen before and certainly never experienced in their own youths. The tone is by turns bossy and breezy, comprehensive (a prom with a May-time theme could include Chocolate Fancies on the refreshment table, and the book provides a recipe), and straightforward: "During the recent years of retrenchment, many schools that have discontinued the junior-senior banquet have substituted the prom." Yet, to the last point, even a cursory glance proves that proms were every bit as expensive as the old banquets, and moreover—where did these schools get the idea for prom?

The sponsoring teacher needed to establish six committees: Decoration Committee, Invitation Committee, Program Committee, Floor Show Committee, Refreshment Committee, and Social Committee. She was to ensure that the students were dressed appropriately for the prom, and to do this she was to consider bringing to a girls-only assembly a person "who dresses in excellent taste herself" and who was "someone who is really authoritative. The main problem with girls' clothing choices for proms is that they tend to overdress," so it was important that the speaker "try to impress on them the beauty and simplicity of youth." They were to be instructed in the beauty of light colors, and that organdies, either printed or plain, "make lovely dresses for girls of this age." Boys could be instructed by the school principal or superintendent, and they were supposed to wear dark trousers, a jacket, a white shirt, and a tie. Just as important was the instruction of the students in special etiquette for prom, which included making sure each one of them approached every single chaperone (all of whom were to be teachers) and offered a formal welcome: "Mrs. Brown, I'm Mary Jones. We are glad you could come to chaperone this evening!"

Where did the girls and their faculty advisers get the raw material for this fanciful production? Not from the formal dances held at the country's elite private schools, which were not called proms, and which had little in common with this new kind of event. Rather, they were inspired by one of the obsessively chronicled and girl-magnetizing phenomena of the Depression: the extravagant coming-out parties of the nation's famous debutantes, the first girl celebrities of the type with which we are all now numbingly familiar, but were then brand-new and riveting. Doris Duke, Barbara Hutton, Eleanor "Cookie" Young, Gloria "Mimi" Baker, Brenda Frazier—all of these girls had their glamorous parties and gorgeous gowns and handsome suitors described around the world, and to the public high school girl, her family scrimping its way through an economic disaster, they were dazzling. Brenda Frazier's 1938 coming-out put her on the cover of *Life* magazine—a girl on the cover of *Life*! For no other reason than that she had been the center of her own glamorous evening party! *Time* magazine wrote that events like hers "provide a glittering view of young women who are launching a career somewhat like that of a cinema star, that of a glamour girl." Brenda Frazier's party, held in the main ballroom of the Ritz-Carlton hotel, featured fifty thousand dollars' worth of entertainment, fifteen hundred guests, and prompted her paternal grandaunt to remark that she abhorred the "spectacular notoriety" of the event. But Brenda's good time had not been daunted by that cutting comment, or by the fact that in a strange, single impetus toward cost-cutting, she had been forced to serve her guests "non vintage champagne." The girls of South Bend Central and Hunter Mountain Consolidated were dazzled by the news that by four thirty in the morning, petulant Brenda had "ended her rhumba dancing and sat down to chat with a table cloth around her shoulders."

The reason that debutante balls, however elaborate, lack the corniness of prom is that they were controlled by adult women—the mothers of the society set, ferociously accomplished hostesses with adamant ideas of what did and did not constitute correct behavior and dress at a formal event and what they wanted their daughters' social aspirations to say about their own place in the world. But in proms we are seeing the desires of America's public high school girls, who were eager to grasp at some of this pageantry for themselves and who were encouraged toward their goal by a variety of forces. In the 1930s, there was a national anxiety that high school was going to feminize boys, that all of these young men who had been bred for work on a farm or in a factory were going to lose their virility because of all the bookishness and seatwork, the recitation of poetry and the study of foreign kings and queens. The answer to this lay principally in sports; to a significant extent, the brutal culture of boys' high school athletics, extant to this day, was created to make sure the boys became men. In concert with this was the assertion of ever more feminine roles for the girls. The twenties flapper, who wouldn't have dreamed of being on the sideline of anything in life, became the thirties cheerleader, breathless supernumerary at the big game.

The prom also had something to offer the parents of these girls: a perfect corrective to the liberation girls had fought for and achieved in the previous decade. With proms, girls were cheerfully submitting themselves to the very forces that so many of them had fought (successfully) to overcome during the 1920s: adult intervention in their romantic lives, careful supervision, protocols centered on notions of restraint, not of liberation. With their hokey themes and elaborate codes of etiquette, proms seemed revolutionary to the girls who invented them, girls who could hardly believe their good luck at having their dreams taken so seriously. But they nonetheless exist in the service of one overriding cultural idea: the notion that courtship should be supervised by adults, conducted in public and shaped around the belief that each girl had one — and no more than one — boy who was right for her. The twenties had given girls dating and heavy petting and liberation, but the thirties worked to take those things away. They suggest that it is possible to put the genie back in the bottle.

Girls were working with their teachers to create a night based on supervision and adult control. Nothing could be more different from the kinds of dates that flappers enjoyed—consisting as they did of a young couple, a car, a few hours of privacy—than a prom, where teachers lurked around the punch bowl, in the shadowed cave under the bleachers, out on the dance floor itself.

Finally, proms gave a means for adults to monitor a force that had become the source of increasing anxiety: dancing. Kelly Schrum, author of *Some Wore Bobby Sox: The Emergence of Teenage Girls' Culture, 1920–1945,* observes that from the beginning of the modern girl movement, "Teenage girls faced many challenges finding appropriate places to dance outside homes." Dance halls, of course, were no places for America's well-raised daughters, and the teen canteens and other postwar dance venues, which were built as a means of controlling the army of unsupervised, after-school teens in the sprawling suburbs, were still decades in the future. And if the places where girls danced were problematic, so too was the way they danced. Schrum notes that in 1914, Shasta Union High School in Redding, California, "forbade students to dance the society walk, that is, up-to-date dances."

Chaperoned, planned, reactionary, and heavily reliant upon the involvement of adults, proms may have represented a step backward in terms of the liberation of girls. But the culture always moves forward as well, and this is true even with the invention of proms. No matter how reactionary they may be, proms nonetheless represent one of the dominant forces of girls' lives in the twentieth century: the weakening of the influence of parents and family over girls, and the growing power of peers and community to shape her life and expectations. In a prom the guidance and standard-setting concerning a girl's romantic life is taken away from the parents and put instead into the hands of a group of public employees, the teachers and administrators of her school, which over the course of the twentieth century would become the seat of her knowledge about everything from menstruation and sexuality to the basics of childrearing and housewifery, which she learned in home economics classes.

"What's happened to prom?" is the question asked every spring, by anxious and excited mothers and by newspaper feature writers looking for easy copy, all of these adults eager to compare their own prom night to those being planned for and by their teenage children—the stretch limos, the stupendously expensive dresses, the once ad hoc after-parties transformed into events as carefully planned and at least as expensive as the proms themselves. Why proms have changed so much is the question on everyone's minds, but the question on my mind is always this: Why have they changed so little? How can it be after all of these years of social upheaval and reconfiguration that when we see a young man—freshly washed, carrying flowers, and dressed in a tuxedo—walking toward a front door, any front door, in early June we know exactly where he is headed: to pick up his prom date, to spend fifteen minutes in a piece of theater he knows because he has seen it so many times in the movies. He'll talk to her parents, express delight at his first sight of her in her gown, stand for pictures, wave good-bye to the dying generation.

In Los Angeles, where I have lived for many years, prom culture reigns supreme. During prom season in Beverly Hills and Brentwood and Encino, the couples still pose for parents' cameras on the green lawns, and the fathers still profess a feeling of bittersweet regret when they first catch sight of their daughters coming down the stairs, transformed into creatures who somehow still evoke their little-girl selves. In Canoga Park (where the average family income is an impressive but nonheady eighty thousand dollars a year), the seniors at the public high school qualify for thirty percent discounts at the local David's Bridal, and they hold their event at Vibiana, a former cathedral of the archdiocese of Los Angeles which has been turned into a wedding and event venue featuring a certain type of gargantuan, enforced elegance. (Vibiana's website boasts, "Whether an intimate party of one hundred, a corporate gathering of a thousand, or any event in between, any guest will be captivated and enchanted by the celebration that surrounds them.") And in all of the blasted suburban cul-de-sacs and security-doored urban apartments in which dwell, however temporarily, the city's roving army of teenagers in foster care, the girls step into the "lightly worn" fancy dresses they have received at a Glamour Gowns event, sponsored by a kindly organization that believes neither "family background nor economic circumstance" should preclude a girl from attending prom.

In America, every girl gets her prom. "Yes, we're in a recession and we're in a bad recession," the owner of a prom dress shop in Tampa told a reporter for the *New York Times* in 2009, after the financial markets collapsed, but the prom business was undimmed: "They're going to forgo other things," she said of the parents who pay the bills, "to make sure their daughter goes to prom." There is some meaning to prom, meaning that unites rich and poor, rural and urban, and even young and old, for who funds the events, ultimately, but aging, former promsters, the parents willing to shortchange themselves almost anything before they will deny a daughter the prom of her dreams. So what, exactly, is the meaning of this event? Why does it have such longevity and engender such sacrifice on the parts of so many?

There are few clues at the proms themselves. Held in hotel ballrooms or fancy catering halls, elaborately decorated and carefully chaperoned by the most popular teachers, the reigning emotion is not one of unbearable excitement at participating in one of life's golden moments. In fact, despite the good music, the big dance floor, the ample buffet table, and the years of anticipation that have funneled down into long months of intense preparation, the emotion is one of boredom. It builds and builds throughout the night. Whatever spasm of excitement may have existed, by the time the clock finally ticks down the last seconds of the event, the kids are often lined up at the exits, which are blocked by teachers, and screaming, "Over! Over! Over!"

The proms, you see, are on lockdown because prom-goers

can no longer be trusted for a minute. Prom night has become an interlude of so much bad behavior—drugs and alcohol and wild sex—that the only way for school administrators to ensure that none of it happens on their watch is to make the kids arrive at a certain time and leave at a certain time and police them every moment in between.

Not since the Hays Code prohibited motion picture makers from depicting childbirth "in fact or in silhouette," as well as excessive kissing, "especially when one character is a 'heavy,'" has there been such a comprehensive and explicit code of conduct as the Downey, California, High School Dance Contract, which kids and their parents must sign before anyone can go to the hop. Signatories understand that there is to be "no touching breasts, buttocks or genitals, no straddling each other's legs. Both feet on the floor." In the Ventura Unified School District, the contract specifies that when "dancing back to front, all dancers must remain upright—no sexual bending is allowed, i.e."—never in the course of English letters has an "i.e." been so desperately needed—"no hands on knees and no hands on the dance floor with your buttocks touching your partner." God, it must be great to be young.

Then again, maybe not, since the kind of dancing these contracts are meant to forbid—and we should solemnly recognize how excruciating it must be for the school administrators who have to compose these things, and who end up essentially creating the educational-bureaucracy version of a pornographic prose poem—is "grinding," which has been all the rage for the last few years, and which is meant to simulate sex. And these are just the challenges that fun-busting administrators of high school *dances* have to confront. Forget about the problems of prom! Nothing says "your very special night" like a fifteen-hundred-dollar Jessica McClintock gown, a Hummer limo, alcohol poisoning, and a "Pimps and Ho's" after-party.

"Over, over, over!" The kids can't wait to get out of prom because they have somewhere far more exciting to go: the after-party. The teachers check the exiting students' names off a list, and in a matter of minutes the corsages and boutonnieres are trampled underfoot, the expensive gowns are smashed down into backpacks and carryalls, new costumes are donned, and the limos and party buses redirected, toward whatever after-hours club or warehouse has been rented out, or whatever huge house has been flushed of its parents and authority figures, and where the red plastic cups and the gallons of strawberry-flavored vodka have been lined up on sticky counters so the real fun can begin. The parties used to have a theme, but now the enforcement of an actual theme has been abandoned in favor of the girls wearing what one teacher I know calls their "slut wear" and the boys getting pimped out.

While prom planning is mostly in the hands of the girls — who labor over the right colors for the table linens and centerpieces, and endlessly vet potential themes and menus — in large part the after-parties are the boys' domain, usually a small cadre with one charismatic leader who fancies himself a promoter and who has an older brother or similar mentor who can help with the logistics of renting out a nightclub, acquiring and transporting to it massive amounts of alcohol (the club owners are fairly rigorous about not selling alcohol to parties of minors), composing a guest list, charging admission, and making a profit. Boys are also in charge of the music, which is almost always sexually explicit. But even if there are no boys on hand to do the planning, a raunchy after-party will follow every prom; I live less than a mile from one of the most respected and prestigious all-girls' schools in the country, an institution from which you can handily vault yourself to the Ivy League, and where every year not only is there a wild after-party but also an annual Pimps and Ho's party so elaborate that it has become a school tradition as venerable and significant as the crowning of incoming students with wreaths made of violets.

While the boys often forgo a special wardrobe of any kind, the girls labor over their outfits. They shop together in groups, at Trashy Lingerie if they have a lot of money to spend, on Halloween-costume websites if they don't. What they end up choosing is a predictable mix of pussycat-dolls and girl-next-door ensembles—lacy bra-and-panty sets, fishnet stockings, high-heeled boots. "We're so crazy," they say to one another when they're getting ready. "Can you believe how crazy we are?" they ask as they jostle off the party buses and onto the sidewalk, where they are regarded with surprised delight by whatever men happen to be there—homeless guys, street thugs, the club's bouncers, wanderers—and who had not expected to get an eyeful of very young, upper-middle-class girls dressed in panties and boots. After one big P&H, held as an after-party to a prom at one of the city's most elite schools and during which a huge number of kids ended up at the emergency room, the girls in their thongs and garters, the boys in their sagging khakis, the parents stormed onto campus wanting to place blame on the administration. But obviously the school was not to blame: it had provided the students with a safe, chaperoned, alcohol-free event, to which the teenagers had arrived dressed to the nines, the boys in tuxes and the girls in party dresses. Where they went after that was between the kids and their parents.

"The number one thing that amazes all of us, year after year," says the dean of students at a private school in Los Angeles, "is the way the parents will let them do absolutely anything on prom night. They will not—I mean *will not*— stop their kids from doing any stupid, dangerous thing they want." One year, she told me, a mother was so frantic about her daughter's plan to attend an after-party that was being held in an abandoned warehouse located in a particularly bleak part of downtown Los Angeles that she made an intervention: not of forbidding the girl to go to the party, but of driving there herself. She spent the whole night sitting in her car outside the warehouse, so that if something happened to her girl—whom she loved beyond life itself, and whom she had spent the past eighteen years nurturing and raising—she would be right there to whisk her to the emergency room.

Clearly the totality of the prom experience—the fancy

dance and the vulgar and wildly sexualized after-party—comprise two equally important sides of a coin that matters a lot to girls. Girls have intentionally combined two events, one composed of traditions that suggest a very formal way of being a teenager, and one composed of behaviors that suggest the exact opposite. There is meaning in these two halves of the equation, in the longing for the past and in the equally strong urge to be part of the present world, even at its ugliest and most humiliating. In this meaning—in the fusing of fantasy and its unvarnished opposite—is Girl Land.

CHAPTER SEVEN

Moral Panics

THE FIRST TIME I heard a mother of girls talk about the teenage oral-sex craze, I made her cry. It was late 2005, when the whole crazy situation—the wild stories, the anguished parents, the horrifying news reports—was reaching its zenith, but somehow I hadn't heard about it yet. The story she told me—about a bar mitzvah dinner dance on the North Shore of Chicago, where the girls serviced all the boys on the chartered bus from the temple to the reception hall—was so preposterous that I burst out laughing. The thought of thirteen-year-old girls in party dresses performing a sex act once considered the province of prostitutes (we are talking here about the on-your-knees variety given to a series of near strangers) was so ludicrous that all I could do was giggle.

It was as though I had taken lightly the news that a pedophile had moved into my friend's neighborhood. It was as though I had laughed about a leukemia cluster or a lethal stretch of freeway. I apologized profusely; I told her I hadn't known. I still thought she was gullible to believe it, but everybody has their one weird thing, and I figured this was hers.

But in the way of these things, not a week had passed before two other women told me similar stories, and in no time at all I realized that a huge number of the moms I knew were convinced—were certain; they knew for a *fact*—that all over the city, in the very best schools, in the nicest families, in the leafiest neighborhoods, twelve- and thirteen-year-old girls were performing oral sex on as many boys as they could. They were ducking into janitors' closets between classes to do it; they were doing it on school buses and in bathrooms, libraries, and stairwells. They were making bar mitzvah presents of the act, and performing it at "train parties": boys lined up on one side of the room, as girls worked their way down the row. I couldn't turn on afternoon or morning television without seeing an earnestly reported and utterly shocking story about the subject. These stories made the average American middle school dude—a kid formerly known for his enthusiasm for video games, tendency to lose his expensive retainer, and inability to bring his math textbook home on two consecutive nights—look like a kind of Hugh Hefner of the eighth grade, enjoying a little oral genital copulation before lumbering off to sixth-period civics. The circle jerk of old—shivering Boy Scouts huddled together in the forest primeval, desperately trying to spank out the first few drops of their own manhood—had apparently moved indoors, and now (death knell of the Eagle Scout?) there's a bevy of girls willing to do the work.

When I first began hearing these tales, I was convinced that we were in the grips of a nationwide urban legend, and the prevalence of stories centered on bar mitzvahs seemed to me suspicious, possibly even anti-Semitic in origin. But when I did a little Googling on the subject, I immediately found something that shocked me: two years earlier, a feminist Jewish quarterly called *Lilith* had addressed the subject— but not to debunk it. Rather the essay asked readers to come to terms with it as a recognized problem within the Jewish community: "No one is suggesting, even for a moment, that Jewish teens are leading the oral sex revolution. But they may have earlier and more frequent opportunities for sexual contact in a supercharged social milieu than their non-Jewish peers." The authors observe that the oral sex is "almost always unilateral (girls on boys)."

In several years of reading and writing about this subject, I have come to understand that the wild stories of group oral sex that seemed to swirl around parents with middle school daughters a few years ago were not accurate. But neither were they the result of pure fabrication. They didn't represent an urban legend, exactly, but rather a moral panic. In 1972 the English sociologist Stanley Cohen published a book called

Folk Devils and Moral Panics, in which he defined a moral panic
as occurring when "a condition, episode, person or group
of persons emerges to become defined as a threat to societal values and interests." He writes, "Because the matter at
the center of these events is always taboo, what unfolds in
response is not rational discourse on the subject, but rather
a frenzy of reaction marked by escalating concern that at
some point coalesces into a consensus opinion or belief—
the point at which a significant number of people stop ques-
tioning whether or not such a threat exists, and accept it as
a proven fact. The cycle is then marked by rapid escalating
hostility and volatility. Moral panics end as mysteriously as
they begin, always with a whimper, not a bang. Sometimes
the threat is slowly but effectively discredited; sometimes a
new one comes to take the place of an old one, its very nov-
elty lending it an urgency that displaces the old fear." In the
post-Clinton era, girls did not begin having depraved oral-
sex parties. But they did develop both a new attitude and a
new set of behaviors regarding oral sex—its role in relationships between boys and girls, its significance, its right place in
the escalating sequence of sexual experiences shared by couples. This change was significant and real, and the response
to it took the form of the escalating panic and hysteria that
marked the era.

The beginning of the oral-sex hysteria can be traced to a single cultural product, something a huge number of American
parents either saw on television or heard described to them.

It turns out that the oral sex panic machine was first switched on by (who would have guessed it?) PBS. In 1999 the network broadcast an episode of *Frontline* that became legendary. Called "The Lost Children of Rockdale County," it centered on a teen syphilis outbreak in Conyers, Georgia, an exurb of Atlanta where vast acres of farmland have been converted into subdivisions of large, handsome houses and where the three local high schools, flush with tax dollars, are among the best in the state. The show became a sensation, was repeatedly rebroadcast, and was featured on *Oprah,* where it was called a "must-see for all parents."

"The Lost Children of Rockdale County" is a bizarre program that takes isolated teen depravity, anxious adult voyeurism, and a dash of venereal disease, and blends them into a vividly yellow piece of public-service journalism—one that typically exaggerates the What, and in so doing just as typically overlooks the Why behind a less sensational but far more pervasive concern. The tale was told largely by middle-aged women who were at turns clinically matter-of-fact about and pruriently fascinated by what happened in Conyers. It turned out that a small group of white girls from stupendously troubled families (yet the kids were described as "cherubic") began meeting in one of the girls' houses after school—and sometimes in a motel room—to do drugs and service two groups of rough trade, one of local white boys, the other of African-American boys (a recent prison inmate among them) who commuted from a different part of the county to avail themselves of the girls. Oral sex wasn't the half of it—what these kids allegedly engaged in combined the degeneracy of a satanic cult with the agility of a Cirque du Soleil troupe. The audience was told that a common after-school activity in Conyers was the "sandwich," in which a girl would be simultaneously penetrated by as many as four boys (the fourth, apparently a Johnny-come-lately, would somehow shoehorn himself into an orifice already occupied by one of his pals). With the kids in Conyers exploiting virtually every known opening for sexual transmission, an outbreak of syphilis was not unlikely. It spread to seventeen students, who were treated and who recovered fully.

But the show also contains interviews with kids who had nothing to do with this horrifying and aberrant episode, kids who seem adrift in the increasingly isolating family culture that was being born in the nineties. They speak of family members who had televisions in their own rooms, who never ate dinner together, who live with one another in the sepulchral McMansions of Conyers the way people live together in hotels: nodding politely as they passed on the stairs, aware of one another's schedules and routines but only in a vague, indifferent manner. These were kids—girls especially—who had developed a dull, curiously passionless relationship to their own sexuality, which they gave of freely. The girls seemed sad that their easily granted sexual favors (including oral sex) had not earned them boyfriends, and they were completely unaware of how they could have negotiated the transactions differently.

The producers ingeniously and dishonorably encourage

the viewer to meld these two stories together, that of the diseased, freaky girls whose behavior represented something genuinely aberrant, and that of the sad, sexually precocious normal kids—in short, to link the activities of the latter with the outcomes of the former. And with this sleight of hand—the suggestion that the behavior of an isolated group of outliers and that of a forlorn but not doomed group of sexually promiscuous suburban girls were one and the same—the seeds of the oral-sex hysteria were officially planted. The belief that casual oral sex in a middle-class school community was an invitation to a teenage public-health threat of epidemic proportions gave the media license to talk about it endlessly and in the most graphic terms imaginable, following the silence = death formulation created during the height of the American AIDS crisis, which encouraged frank public sexual discourse in the hope of saving lives. It's a no-miss formula: descriptions of young girls performing oral sex which are so luridly specific as to seem pedophilic in the adults' retelling, coupled with stern warnings to parents that their daughters are in harm's way.

Four months after the *Frontline* documentary aired, *Talk* magazine published an essay called "The Sex Lives of Your Children." Its author, Lucinda Franks, described an upper-middle-class white world in which oral sex began at age twelve, and said—in perhaps the first published use of the term—that train parties abounded. For the sake of journalistic accuracy she reported a twelve-year-old girl's description of the taste of sperm, and during an NPR radio interview about her essay she referred to the Conyers incident in the wildly inaccurate way in which the episode had quickly passed into the national consciousness: in Rockdale County, Georgia, "a whole town—the kids came down with syphilis."

The story burned its way into the national consciousness. Two years after the broadcast, in 2001, Oprah invited Dr. Phil to appear on her television show to address the topic. "There's an oral-sex epidemic," Oprah told the audience while teary mothers related their horrifying stories. "A year or two ago she was playing with Barbies and collecting Beanie Babies. And then now all of a sudden she's into casual oral sex!" Wide-eyed young girls spilled the beans on their slutty classmates and intimated that they themselves weren't so different. That the entire subject is ugly and fraught was underscored when Dr. Phil decided to confront a young blow-jobber about the error of her ways. She was sitting in the front row next to her mother, who was apparently hoping that public humiliation on a global scale might reform her daughter.

Dr. Phil, who employs a psychotherapeutic cloak of respectability to legitimize his many prurient obsessions, harangued her. "When you're saying, 'It's just friends,' let me tell you," he raged at the poor girl, "a friend doesn't ask you to go in the bathroom, get on your knees on a urine-splattered tile floor, and stick their penis in your mouth. That's not what I call a friend."

As the audience roared its approval (whether for chastity or obscenity was unclear), the girl looked stricken and angry.

"That's not what happened to me," she whispered audibly to her mother, who whispered back, *"Tell him."* But the girl was understandably cowed by the specter of Dr. Phil on one of his verbal stampedes, and she said nothing, leaving him clueless about a major aspect of the oral-sex craze. No boy had forced the girl anywhere. In all likelihood she herself had been the initiator, the location scout, the one who had decided that this was indeed an activity that could take place between two "friends." (The oral-sex hysteria has attributed to American boys not only superhuman virility but also wanton emotional cruelty. The one is laughable; the other in the main is just not the case. Like the medical dodge, the demonization of boys oversimplifies the problem and spares one the arguably sadder truth.)

In 2003 Oprah addressed the topic again: "Parents, brace yourselves." Teenagers were leading "double lives"—and we all needed to get hip to the code words they used. The journalist who wrote a related article for *O* magazine got right to the point: A "tossed salad," for example, was "oral sex to the anus." A "dirty" girl was a diseased one. And a "rainbow party" was a blow-job party where the girls wore different-colored lipstick.

Apparently taking a break from her toil in the vineyard of belles lettres—relaxing, in fact, by watching *Oprah*—was a woman named Bethany Buck, a Simon & Schuster editrix who smelled a winner. She contacted a writer named Paul Ruditis (one of whose previous books was *The Brady Bunch Guide to Life*); together they created characters and an outline, and he was sent off to type the thing up. The product was a novel called *Rainbow Party,* and the tale it told was so outlandish and ridiculous that it not only became a media sensation, but it ended up performing an unlikely public service: by simply describing, earnestly and in detail, the nature of a group oral-sex party held by teenagers, it revealed how ridiculous such a notion really is, and thereby served to calm the raging anxieties of millions of parents.

Rainbow Party takes place on a single day, in which a tough little sophomore named Gin issues invitations to a party at which she and five of her friends will perform oral sex on the lucky guests, a group of popular boys. The girls will each wear a different color of lipstick, so that when a boy has completed the circuit, his penis will bear the colors of the rainbow. The party is to take place after school, to last about an hour and a half—including time for chitchat—and to conclude before Gin's father returns home from work.

In addition to the predictable, outraged criticism this vile book received, there is a question of veracity: as many readers noted, wouldn't the different colors of lipstick smear together, destroying the desired rainbow effect? Not once, however, was another question posed: How many boys could successfully receive seven blow jobs in an hour? Surely even the adolescent male at the peak of his sexual prime needs at least a few minutes to reload. One would assume that the first transaction would be completed at lightning speed, that the second might take a bit longer...and that by the fourth or fifth even the horniest tenth grader might display some real staying power. But asking questions like these would automatically preclude you from entering the oral-sex hysteria, which presupposes not only that a limitless number of young American girls took on the sexual practices of porn queens, but also that American boys are capable of having an infinite number of sexual experiences in rapid succession. It requires believing that a boy could be serviced at the school-bus train party—receiving oral sex from ten or fifteen girls, one after another—and then zip his fly and head off to homeroom, first stopping in the stairwell for a quickie to tide him over until math.

Rainbow Party has the feeling of true pornography. In particular, it has the feeling of homosexual-male pornography. The school is called Harding High, and the prose takes a quickening, vivid leap forward when two boys, Hunter and Perry, duck into the school bathroom, where Perry services his pal and then wonders if they might be gay. Otherwise the book is inert, obscene without being erotic, its slim narrative structure insufficient for the gimmickry of its premise. The party is eventually undermined by a series of debacles, leaving Gin and her pal Sandy alone to service the crowd—and then the boys can't even be bothered to show up. This is clearly a high school humiliation of an entirely new and apocalyptic order. What if you gave a blow-job party but nobody came? Injury to insult, Gin gets the clap, victim and catalyst of a school-wide gonorrhea outbreak.

The book's sole effective literary technique is achieved unintentionally: *Rainbow Party* is so leaden and formulaic, so

completely deadened to any of the possibilities of fiction, that
it mirrors the way girls are said to feel about fellatio—jaded
and shockproof. (It's not just Hunter and Perry's high jinks
in the restroom that put one in mind of bathhouse culture.
Almost everything about the blow-job craze—the random-
ness of the sexual encounters, the fact that they're apparently devoid of meaning beyond the immediate gratification
of male desire, that neither party is inclined to say "no," that
little consideration is given to female desire, or even female
anatomy—suggests a strain of gay male sex more than it does
traditional male-female relationships.) It is hard to imagine
that a person could read a novel like that and feel genuine
emotion of any kind. Because *Rainbow Party* presented such a
ridiculous vision, because it received so much media attention
and was built on a premise that was so easily and quickly de-
bunked, it helped to end the hysteria around kids and oral-sex
parties. Orgiastic episodes were blessedly rare, but still there
was a real change—one that was far less sensational in nature, but nonetheless profound—in young people's attitudes
toward and behavior regarding oral sex.

No, there weren't real-life rainbow parties. But parents,
school administrators, teachers, parents, and girls can all confirm a major shift in modern sexual habits and expectations.
Fellatio, which was once a part of the sexual repertoire of
only experienced women, is now commonly performed by
very young girls outside of romantic relationships, casually
and without any expectation of reciprocation.

It used to be that a hopeful recipient of fellatio had a lot of talking to do—to persuade, and very often to instruct, his partner. (*The Sensuous Woman,* published in 1969, was shocking for a number of reasons, but most of all because it gave to its audience of middle-class women explicit instructions on how to perform oral sex. "Now don't turn up your nose and make that ugly face!" says the anonymous author, "J." Oral sex is the "preferred way with many movie stars, artists, titled Europeans and jet setters.")

Nowadays girls don't consider oral sex in the least exotic—nor do they even consider it to be sex. It's just "something to do." A friend who attended a leadership conference for girls from some of the country's top schools told me, "Friendships haven't changed a bit since our day. But sex has changed *a lot.*" One of the teachers, from an eastern boarding school, told the students that when she was young, in the 1960s, oral sex was considered far more intimate than intercourse. The kids hooted at the notion. "It's like licking a lollipop," one pretty girl from a prestigious girls school said, flipping her hair in the ancient gesture of teenage certainty. "It's no big deal." Somehow, in a very short period of time, girls developed an indifferent attitude toward performing oral sex.

During a casual visit I made to the Info for Teens section of Planned Parenthood's website, I found a trove of information for adolescents on the topics of not only vaginal but also oral and anal sex, including detailed information on how to perform these acts.

At the time, Info for Teens included lots of helpful information from a woman at Rutgers University who is named Nora Gelperin, but who goes by the moniker the "Oral Sex Lady." Nora (who is the recipient of the 2010 Mary Lee Tatum Award from the Association of Planned Parenthood Leaders in Education) digs her job, which involves analyzing attitudes about oral sex. She does offer some tips for those who want to curb the oral-sex trend: they should have bull sessions with groups of kids to "illuminate the variety of teens' opinions about oral sex," in order to "more accurately reflect the range of opinions instead of continuing to propagate the stereotype that 'all teens are having oral sex.'" In other words, instead of the adult instructing kids in what is right and wrong and telling them what is expected of them, the kids themselves should seek direction from one another. A mother concerned that her daughter has turned to performing oral sex on strangers at age twelve should bear this in mind: "We must not forget that the desire of early adolescents to feel sexual pleasure is normal and natural and should be celebrated, not censored."

In recent years, public health studies devoted to understanding teen sexual behavior have switched from the question of whether girls are more often performing oral sex on their boyfriends than in years past to the question of why this might be the case. When trying to understand any act of teens' behavior, you can never underestimate the sheer desire to break boundaries, to explore shocking new territories never even imagined by your parents. If Mom and Dad are having a half-philosophical, half-prurient conversation about oral sex, prompted by a headline in *USA Today*, while you're trying to eat a bowl of Frosted Mini-Wheats and review your spelling words, the concept of oral sex is going to seem a lot less mysterious and boundary-breaking when you're thirteen and fourteen and fifteen years old.

For every Clinton-basher who wanted to blame Bill for the private sexual practices of America's post-Monica teen girls, there was someone on the other side of the political spectrum eager to blame the kind of abstinence-only sex education promulgated by conservatives, which gave millions of kids the idea that vaginal intercourse was to be avoided at all costs, and therefore made oral sex more attractive. Planned Parenthood seems almost to advocate oral sex among the young, a fact underscored by their antipathy toward abstinence-only programs.

"Why has oral sex become so popular?" asks Info for Teens. Well, one reason is because girls want to remain "technical virgins": "In abstinence education, you learn that you should stay a virgin," says Matt, fifteen. "So if you have oral sex, you don't have to lose your virginity, and you don't feel like you are doing something as bad."

Matt isn't the only teen who thinks oral sex "doesn't count." A Columbia University study found that teens who took virginity pledges were more likely to have anal and oral sex than teens who didn't pledge. Pledgers were substituting these other kinds of sex play for vaginal sex in order to stay "technical virgins," an interesting proposition, although I would hardly count Columbia as the go-to source for information on the hearts and minds of evangelical Christian teenagers.

Wherever there's a girl gone wild, there's a gender studies professor not far behind, eager to blame her actions on the patriarchy. One of these is Julian Carter, formerly at NYU, now at the California College of the Arts, who says that oral sex among young teen girls is part of a complex power dynamic, one that is familiar to people who know how Carol Gilligan's influential book *In a Different Voice* has dominated feminist thinking. Says Carter: "It's precisely at this age of early adolescence that...girls' sense of self-worth changes dramatically...this is when they are finding out they have less power within a patriarchal system." According to Carter's theory, the girls are apparently suffering from a severe form of Stockholm syndrome and have reacted by performing oral sex on their wily captors.

The problem with this idea is that surely the patriarchy was far stronger and more oppressive in the 1950s. But you don't find Betty—or even Veronica—cravenly servicing Archie and Jughead. Indeed, during the very years that the patriarchy has been most seriously eroded, we have seen a cult of mortification of the flesh take root among teenage girls. The anorexia and bulimia that swept the teen population in the eighties, the "cutting" fad of the nineties, and now this strange new preference for unreciprocated oral sex all evolved as the patriarchy was being crippled, as new and untested roles were being offered to the country's girls.

* * *

For me, the most shocking moment in "The Lost Children of Rockdale County"—more shocking even than the "sandwich"—involves three giggly blond best friends forever who give an extensive, girly interview while sitting in one of their bedrooms, surrounded by stuffed animals. At a certain point one of the producers asks them what kind of music they like, and they all squeal, "Rap!" The coaxing producer says, "Give me an example." The girls decide to sing for her, and their sweet, piping voices flow easily over the lyrics, which they all know by heart—three teenyboppers sitting in a suburban bedroom, singing their favorite song, "Love in Ya Mouth," the lyrics of which I will spare you, but the content of which is a long, single-entendre meditation on the joys of making girls perform oral sex and then casting them aside.

One of the most astonishing things to happen during the 1990s was that rap music that included some of the most violent, sexually explicit, and misogynistic lyrics ever recorded slipped seamlessly and virtually unnoticed into the households of so many apparently responsible American families. Boomer parents, remembering their own struggles with their square parents over rock and roll, were lenient about their kids' music. Tipper Gore's heroic campaign to get explicit music rated and labeled was born after she decided to do something few parents had even attempted: actually listen to the albums her kids had bought. She was ridiculed by many factions, including those forces on the American left who cry censorship whenever anyone attempts to protect the public, including children, from smut (and in the case of rap, smut emanating from a source the left valorizes: black urban America). In the summer of 2004 Bill Cosby brought down a hail of criticism when he lambasted the hip-hop culture as a shameful squandering of the civil rights gains that his generation had fought for and won.

But the protests of white senators' wives and African-American senior citizens have not had much effect on music sales, and have not prevented a large number of poor and middle-class kids alike from becoming saturated by the world of spoken-word, hard-core pornography that is rap music. Add to this the countless other products of our increasingly sexualized teen culture, in which male sexual fantasy of the type once reserved for prison-yard posturing has been adopted and championed by very young girls who stand only to be brutalized by it—emotionally, if not physically.

Ironically, many of the objectives stated in rap lyrics are the same as those of contemporary American feminism: to encourage girls not to be shackled by the double standard and to abandon modesty as a goal, to erode patriarchal notions of how men ought to treat women, and to champion aggressiveness in girls. It was very possible for a girl in the nineties to have her well-intentioned parents buy her a CD in which she was urged to suck dick and get fucked, and to have a well-intentioned teacher (I was one such) tell her to be as intellectually and verbally aggressive as she could—that aggression for its own sake was a good thing, because it leveled the playing field in a male-dominated world.

At the same time, actual pornography—once the province of the most marginalized and criminally suspect performers and businessmen; once a slice of illicit commerce entirely beyond the purview of decent society—was entering the mainstream. It became possible to find porn star Jenna Jameson discussing her trade with the likes of Anderson Cooper on CNN. It was possible, furthermore, to discover that she was being interviewed not as a fallen woman but as a successful businessperson. Simultaneously, feminists were turning themselves into pretzels trying to get together a coherent policy on pornography. Obviously it was exploitative—unless it wasn't. Because if it was explicit sexual material made for the arousal of women, then it was somehow...empowering? And how to deal with the Jenna Jamesons of the world, who were proving themselves to be feminist powerhouses, keeping the government out of private decisions about their own bodies (thank you, abortion rhetoric!) and profiting handsomely from the results?

When I was in eleventh grade, I invited a new boyfriend to come to my house after school one day. My mother was outside gardening, or maybe she was on the telephone, or reading—she was around, but through a glass. The boy and I made Top Ramen at the stove, and afterward I invited him to come up to my bedroom. I had never been told not to do such a thing; I seemed then to be lacking a lot of clear information about what I could and could not do. My parents were preoccupied at the time with other things. I was the youngest girl in a daughter-raising project that they appeared to think had gone terribly wrong. They were no longer giving the enterprise their full oomph.

In the bedroom the atmosphere was charged. I remember that he sat on my Pier 1 wicker chair, and that I showed him my wall calendar, which had a different, adorable kitten for each month. And then, abruptly, I said that we should go back downstairs, and he stood—immediately—and followed me. At the foot of the stairs we found my mother, looking as though she had been close to charging up.

"Never bring a boy to your bedroom," she told me afterward.

"Why not?"

There was a fumbling for words, and then an answer: "Because he might go to school and tell other boys what your comforter looks like."

It was a white Dior comforter with yellow rosebuds and matching sheets. The bed was a Sears four-poster princess bed, a little-girl's bed, but we had taken off the canopy and added the Dior linens to dress it up. I had wanted pink roses, but the pink had not gone on sale at the El Cerrito Capwell's. The yellow had.

"That's so *stupid*," I yelled at my mother. "Just so completely *stupid!*" She sighed wearily—the raising-girls sigh, the sigh of bottomless despair. Why hadn't she thrown herself off the Golden Gate Bridge at last opportunity? Why had she ever been so foolish as to think it was good news each time the obstetrician told her she had been delivered of a girl?

But even in my teenage snit I understood what she was talking about: Not the comforter but my reputation. Not the boy himself (who was a very nice person—anyone could tell it just from meeting him) but the immutable truth about boys. They want most what we keep private. When it's known, it's lessened.

At the time of my adolescence my mother was too distracted to give me everything I needed to turn out well. But 20 percent of her attention was enough, because the whole culture was supporting her. The notion that a girl should not give her sexuality away too freely was so solidly built into the national consciousness that my mother didn't have to snap out of her depression and give me a comprehensive lecture on boys for me to understand what she meant. It was a period when artists and entertainers and commercial America in general did not have untrammeled access to the country's youth. Television shows were heavily censored, as were radio stations. George Carlin's "Seven Words You Can Never Say on Television" was hilarious not just for its string of bad words but because of the context in which he invited us to imagine their use: think of turning on the network TV and hearing the word "fuck"! Sex ed in those days was a little like driver's ed: a grimly delivered set of facts, copiously illustrated with hideous examples of what could go wrong if you were foolhardy enough to operate the machinery. ("Is there going to be a test?" a girl asked about the contraception unit. "Your life is the test," she was told.) At the time, feminists were distracted by the vast project of American womanhood; they had not yet turned their attention to the country's girls.

As a parent, I am horrified by the changes that have taken place in the common culture over the past thirty years. I believe that we are raising children in a kind of postapocalyptic landscape in which no forces beyond individual households—individual mothers and fathers—are protecting children from pornography and violent entertainment. The "it takes a village" philosophy is a joke, because the village is now so polluted and so desolate of commonly held, child-appropriate moral values that my job as a mother is not to rely on the village but to protect my children from it.

I'm not, however, terrified by the oral-sex craze. If I were to learn that my children had engaged in oral sex—outside a romantic relationship, and as young adolescents—I would be sad. But I wouldn't think that they had been damaged by the experience; I wouldn't think I had failed catastrophically as a mother, or that they would need therapy. Because I don't have daughters, I have sons.

I am old-fashioned enough to believe that men and boys are not as likely to be wounded, emotionally and spiritually, by early sexual experience, or by sexual experience entered into without romantic commitment, as are women and girls. I think that girls are vulnerable to great damage through the kind of sex in which they are, as individuals, as valueless and unrecognizable as chattel. Society has let its girls down in every possible way. It has refused to assert—or even to acknowledge—that female sexuality is as intricately connected to kindness and trust as it is to gratification and pleasure. It's in the nature of who we are.

But perhaps the girls themselves understand this essential truth.

As myriad forces were combining to reshape our notions of public decency and propriety, to ridicule the concept that privacy and dignity are valuable and allied qualities of character and that exhibitionism as an end in itself might not be beneficial for a young girl, at the exact moment when girls were encouraged to think of themselves as victims of an oppressive patriarchy and to act on an imperative of default aggression—at this very time a significant number of young girls were beginning to form an entirely new code of sexual ethics and expectations. It was a code in which their own physical pleasure was of no consequence—was in fact so entirely beside the point that their preferred mode of sexual activity was performing unrequited oral sex. *Deep Throat* lingers in the popular imagination because it was one of the few porn movies to trade on an original and inspired premise: what a perfect world it would be if the clitoris were located in a woman's throat. In a world like that, a man wouldn't have to cajole a woman to perform fellatio on him; she would be just as eager to get it on as he was. But this was a fantasy; a girl may derive a variety of consequences, intended and otherwise, from servicing boys in this manner, but her own sexual gratification is not one of them.

The modern girl's casual willingness to perform oral sex may—as some coolheaded observers of the phenomenon like to propose—be her way of maintaining a postfeminist power in her sexual dealings, by being fully in control of the sexual act and of the pleasure a boy receives from it. Or it may be her desperate attempt to do something that the culture refuses to encourage: to keep her own sexuality—the emotions and the desires, as well as the anatomical real estate itself—private, secret, unviolated. It may not be her technical virginity that she is trying to preserve; it may be her own sexual awakening—which is all she really has left to protect anymore.

Culture and Counterculture

Girls are powerfully drawn to the popular culture of their age, which they find mesmerizing and enticing. The overweening nature of adolescence, the sense of invulnerability, the certainty that you are wiser and more independent than you actually are, the complete ignorance of what has come before you, which fuels your convictions — of authenticity, of originality — this is what propels teenagers forward, often uncritically, into the cultural fashions being shaped for them. For adults today, the Internet-driven, pornography-centered popular culture to which our teenagers are so deeply attracted is a mystery, fathomless and dark. It troubles us and emanates from places so foreign that it seems like a rupture from all that has come before, but it's not; it is part of a continuum. Every generation pushes the boundary of acceptable behavior a little further out.

But make no mistake: the mass media in which so many girls are immersed today does not mean them well; it is driven by a set of priorities largely created by men and largely devoted to the exploitation of girls and young women. Even a teenage girl who doesn't seem particularly interested in the current culture is not safe from it, because the culture is interested in her. It encourages her to think of herself as a creature who lives to please men, to post revealing or undignified photographs of herself online, to develop a persona on Facebook and Twitter that is highly sexual. It wants her to live her private moments in public, to expose every aspect of her interior life for all to see, to dress and behave in ways that will draw the most heated reactions from boys and men. The question parents of girls must ask themselves is to what extent they want their daughters raised within this culture, and to what extent they want to raise them within a counterculture that rejects the commercialization of sexuality, the imperatives toward exhibitionism and crudeness. Creating a counterculture is hard work, but it can be done, and it is my strong belief that the young women who emerge from Girl Land having been protected from the current mainstream values are much stronger and more self-confident than those who have been immersed in it throughout their adolescences. What follows are some thoughts and recommendations on how to achieve this for your own daughter.

1. Take the Fifteen-Minute Tour

The nature of culture is progressive and cumulative. Each generation of young people faces an essentially remade world. But despite this obvious fact, parents are deeply ambivalent about, or outright unwilling, to limit their daughters' access to the wide world of the Internet, which they have accepted, with resignation, as an aspect of modern life which their daughters must navigate as best they can. The same mothers who read every book they can get their hands on about girls and self-esteem, and who fret endlessly about mean girls and teasing, will allow their daughters to go online without any supervision, to go to slumber parties at houses where there are computers but no rules about using them, to have cell phones with Internet access. I would say to every parent of an adolescent girl who is about to make decisions about her access to the various new forms of technology: take the Fifteen-Minute Tour, and do so through the eyes of your young daughter. Set a timer for a quarter of an hour and type the word "porn" into your search engine. This, obviously, is not a term most young adolescent girls will search for, but it will take you most expeditiously to the places that their innocent search terms will quickly take them to. The same impulse that led a previous generation of girls to pore over purloined copies of *Playboy* magazine when they had slumber parties—curiosity, bravado, the thrill of initiating a new girl into the fold of secret knowledge—leads them to go looking for representations of adult sexuality on the Internet. But the scope of the Hugh Hefner enterprise, as shocking and titillating as it may have been to the young teenagers of previous decades, bears as much resemblance to the fetish pornography of today's online world as an actual bunny farm did to a Hefner club.

By minute two you are probably witnessing events that are far afield from the mutually satisfying exploits of *Forever,* and by minute three you are watching events that have an obvious aspect of assault. What does a twelve- or thirteen- or fourteen-year-old girl make of these nonstop images? Why are so many adults so quick to say that contemporary pornography is not of any substantive difference from the old copies of *Playboy* that kids of an earlier generation stumbled across? I doubt any parent can take the Fifteen-Minute Tour and decide that there's no reason to shield a young daughter from it, and I would suggest that any decisions you make about your girl and technology be informed by what you have seen.

The sophisticated, politically correct attitude about pornography is that it offers women a way of capitalizing on male erotic desire, and that feeling sympathy for the women involved in the business is patronizing. The truth about pornography is that the majority of women on camera who are paid for their work were sexually abused as children or teenagers, have had serious problems with drugs and alcohol, and are often loaded on the days of shooting. You are probably looking at images that devolve from an attitude toward women that is contemptuous and that to young girls is terrifying.

Think about how many young teenage girls have already

taken the Fifteen-Minute Tour. Think about all of the millions of girls in this country who have an Internet connection in their bedrooms, and have far greater abilities than you and I will ever have to circumvent the Net Nannys and other parental controls that their mothers and fathers assumed would keep them safe.

2. Make her bedroom an Internet-free zone

The most obvious reason to do this, of course, is to protect her from the kind of pornography described above. But the equally important reason is to defend Girl Land as a private space and time for a girl to think and dream and where she can be completely free from the influence of friends and peers. The constant incursion of the cell phone and instant messaging, the round-the-clock, deeply addictive, and anxiety-producing gossip mill of the social networking sites that teens love, are a drain on the energy needed in Girl Land. Parents are wise to help daughters carve out some space and time where no one can get to them, and where they can have refuge. Surfing the Net, as we have all discovered, can become an all-consuming, addictive behavior, one that leaves no space for dreaming or creativity. An hour or two can go by, and it's as though your mind has been taken prisoner as your fingers click and click away, taking in only information and images, never having a moment of critical or imaginative thought. This is exactly the kind of thought that is so important in Girl

Land, and it is why a girl's room needs to be defended as a sanctuary.

Taking away the Internet connection in her bedroom is one of the greatest gifts a parent can give a daughter, but it's one she won't thank you for in the short term. The first thing she will tell you is that she needs her computer so she can do her homework, but in my experience the number of minutes teenagers actually need to be online studying or researching on any given night is negligible compared to the amount of time they spend surfing and chatting. She can do her online homework in a common area of the house.

3. Get her father involved in her dating life

Fathers are crucial in the lives of adolescent girls, because when a daughter grows up with an involved, caring father at home with her, she has already solved one of the big questions of the female experience: am I capable of loving and being loved by an adult male? She is not looking to her dating life to provide her with an answer to that question, and she is less likely to be attracted to boys who are much older than she is, or boys who would treat her poorly. A father at home is also invaluable to adolescent girls because it makes them far less likely to be targets of the kind of boys who become emotionally, physically, or sexually abusive. Those kinds of teenage boys are punks, and the one thing punks can't stand is coming under the authority and scrutiny of a powerful adult male.

In the early days of dating, far more girls lived with their fathers than do now, and the results of this changing demographic are partly revealed in the incidence of teen dating violence: with no man deeply invested in her sexual and personal safety standing as a shield between her and the teenage boys who want to spend time alone with her, the possibility of things going poorly on the date increase. If her father is not in the picture, some other older male relative should perform this role, an uncle or grandfather or stepfather.

4. Remember: giving a girl limits doesn't limit the girl

Many parents are afraid that if they raise their daughters differently from their sons, providing more protection and limits for girls than for boys, they will shortchange the girl. But the reverse is true—Girl Land is a finite period of emerging identity, one that can feel confusing and frightening. If her parents take care to protect her during this time, to keep her safe from the forces that seek to exploit or diminish her, she will be stronger and more confident as a woman than if she had been set adrift in the culture without special safeguards.

5. Girl Land ends

Parents dread the arrival of Girl Land, because during this time their beloved daughters seem to disappear. They retreat, become sullen, vanish right in front of you and then come zinging back to life—giggling, expressing outsize emotions, being embarrassed by every little thing—when they are around their friends. You have to remember: Girl Land ends, and the person you've always known and loved will come back to you. But you must also know this: she will be changed.

Epilogue

My FATHER WAS A scholar and historian, one of those charismatic professors who forever had a coterie of graduate students and young academics pressed around him, sometimes literally sitting at his feet. My mother was a former nurse who had left work to raise children and keep house. It was along these broad strokes of character that the general story of their marriage, of our family, was understood: the absentminded intellectual who had never even learned to drive a car, his capable wife who managed the practicalities of their lives. He was respected; she was loved.

The truth was more complicated than that, of course, but the old story reasserted itself even on the day of my mother's memorial service. Thanking the crowd of assembled guests, my father observed how many poets had made the journey to honor her.

"Jean liked poets," he said, thoughtfully, and then—with a sudden gleam in his eye—he added, "although she didn't like poetry."

It got a laugh, and it seemed to me a perfect remark, in that it managed to convey, in an economy of words, the exact nature of his relationship with her and toward her: it suggested fondness, condescension, exaggerated bewilderment, and willful dishonesty. My mother, in fact, loved poetry, and anyone who knew her well—certainly anyone who had lived with her—knew that for a fact. She knew lots of complicated poems by heart, especially ones that could delight children, like "Jabberwocky" and "The Children of Lir." She knew more Yeats than most people with advanced degrees in English. But there was no poem she loved better or recited more often than Hopkins's "Spring and Fall."

How many times was I near her—sitting in the passenger seat at a red light, setting the table while she peeled potatoes, lurking on the front porch while she stood looking at the sunset, a cigarette or glass of wine in her hand—when suddenly, out of nowhere, like someone thinking out loud, she would ask, "Margaret, are you grieving, over Goldengrove unleaving?"

If my father was also on the scene, he would jump right in, supplying the ready answer to her question, sometimes both of them saying the fateful words together: "It is the blight man was born for, It is *Margaret* you mourn for."

If you were a cool-eyed adolescent daughter, carefully cat-aloguing each of the ways your parents disappointed you—with particular attention, in the way of adolescent daughters everywhere, to the exact shortcomings of your mother—the "Spring and Fall" duets gave you pause. They almost always ended with a bit of physical affection from my father to my mother—he would put his arm around her, or give her shoulder a little squeeze. And most interesting of all, my mother would often betray, in her expression, or the slump of her shoulders, a bit of vulnerability, such a rare emotion for her. Tenderness between them was rare and significant. "Spring and Fall" is a mournful poem, no doubt about it, but the charge of sentiment and fellow-feeling which it seemed to engender in my parents seemed larger than poetry alone.

It's a short poem about the biggest subjects: human suffering and mortality. And the improbable, perfect metaphor for these lofty themes is the wrenching act of a young child leaving her girlhood behind and coming to terms with all of the bittersweet realities that are at the heart of Girl Land. Margaret, the girl of such exquisite sensitivities, such keen apprehension of impending loss, may flatter herself that what is grieving her is the end of sylvan playland, laid waste by another autumn, that she is a person whose exaggerated sympathies can extend even to the turning leaves in the trees. But of course, it isn't Goldengrove she's really mourning; it's her own loss of little girlhood, the fleeting moments of being at once close enough to it and far enough away from it to realize just how dear and how great and unrecoverable a loss she is sustaining.

They had their moments, my mother and father. I'll give them that. They were people who got noticed. They were famous for their dinner parties and for the scope of my father's wit and imagination, and for my mother's easy, confident way around so many different kinds of people. Everyone's parents must have been beautiful when they were young, but I have seen a few old photographs of mine in their early days together, and by any objective standard they were a couple of very good-looking kids, making a go of it during an exciting time. They were young in New York during the exact moment that everyone wishes they were young in New York. Even now, after so many decades of trying to see them for who they really were, the legend asserts itself: the young man who walked from his dormitory at Amherst to the naval recruiting station in town on December 8, 1941, and the girl in nursing school so beautiful they took her photograph for a poster. Depression kids who started with so little but who, toward the end, drank gin and tonics together at the Danieli. I've seen the photograph of the two of them there—ravaged by time, two old folks thrilled with their luck—holding glasses. Although I wasn't there, I can tell you with certainty what he said to her when they clinked them together: "Stick with me, kid."

But nothing had been to them as significant or as happy or as consonant with their deepest emotional needs as having two little girls in the house. For my mother, the project of having these daughters, one a quiet helper and thoughtful companion, the other a chatterbox and minor villain, was such a perfect fulfillment of such a deep longing that she was too enraptured by it to realize it was going to come to an end. She was a woman who never recovered from losing her own mother as a little girl, and who had never believed that it would be possible to recapture the lost world—the dress-up box and the fairy plays and the long evenings sitting together in the rocking chair—until there it was again, complete.

My sister and I launched ourselves from home the way people of our generation did: convulsively and completely, and also with a kind of scorched-earth finality that was the product of the particular times we grew up in and of the intensity of the family drama we were desperate to escape. But whether we had done it more gently or more languorously, the result of our leaving would have been the same: no matter how we accomplished it, we would have broken our mother's heart.

And I realize now, far too late to do anything about it, that what prompted all those sudden recitations of "Spring and Fall," all those moments of wistful vulnerability and marital closeness, wasn't the red light or the dinner preparation or the beauty of a Golden Gate sunset. It was the apparent supernumerary in the scene, the girl in the bucket seat who had her eye on the stoplight and her heart set on an imminent departure. There wasn't anything any one of us could have done to forestall the end of Girl Land, and we got over it, we made it up to each other, but it was never the same again between us. It never is for anyone.

"I want you to have these," my mother said to me suddenly, one night in my kitchen, a few weeks before she died. I was too young then to understand that if someone abruptly gives away the things she loves the most, she is telling you something important.

What she gave me that busy night were the two hollow gold bracelets her own mother had worn, and that she herself wore every day that I knew her, the ones that clink together in such a particular way, reminding me so powerfully of how they would clink together when she was turning a page in *Little House on the Prairie,* or brushing my hair, or zipping up one of my dresses, so that even now, so many years later, they are in two separate pouches in the back of a drawer so that I never have to hear that sound again.

I don't have any daughters, and there isn't anyone who will be bucking to inherit the bracelets on their own merits; I bet together they're not worth more than fifty dollars. I don't have any idea what will happen to them after I die. Probably someone will come across them and realize, because of the care with which they have been put aside, that they ought to be passed down. Almost certainly—it only makes sense— they will be separated.

A Note on Sources

The literature of Girl Land is rich, and in writing this book I read not only histories and biographies related to the subject; I also immersed myself in the books and movies and television shows of my own girlhood, to recall the intense emotional reactions I had to them. I reread books that centered on the progress of a girl, such as *A Tree Grows in Brooklyn* and *Joy in the Morning* by Betty Smith, *Mrs. Mike* by Benedict and Nancy Freedman, the Laura Ingalls Wilder series, and also the novels that were pressed upon young teenagers of my era as cautionary tales, books such as *Mr. and Mrs. Bo Jo Jones* and *Too Bad About the Haines Girl,* which were about nice girls who went too far with their boyfriends and ended up as teenage mothers. I reread the anti–drug scare novels, like *Go Ask Alice* and the ones that were supposed to show you how to keep an overeager boy at bay, like Paul Zindel's *My Darling, My Hamburger.* And of course I read the sensible, optimistic novels of Judy Blume, which were among the most important girl texts of my era, *Are You There God? It's Me, Margaret* and *Forever.* I also reread some of the racy novels written for adults that had affected me as a girl, like *Goodbye, Columbus* and *Valley of the Dolls.* And the novels foisted on girls by adults, *The Bell Jar* and *Island of the Blue Dolphins.*

I acquired and pored over a second kind of literary output: old high school yearbooks, endless back issues of *Seventeen* and *Young Miss* magazines, and girls autograph books, which I began collecting. I bought old Camp Fire Girl and Girl Scout guidebooks—the ones written for girls and also the ones written for troop leaders—and I got hold of a stupendous number of facsimile editions of brochures produced by the makers of sanitary products and aimed at young girls, available at an invaluable online resource called the Museum of Menstruation.

The subject of girls history, as distinct from women's history or adolescent history in general, has become a significant field of inquiry, and I am grateful in particular to the books of Joan Jacobs Brumberg, *The Body Project* and *Fasting Girls,* as well as to Crista DeLuzio's work *Female Adolescence in American Scientific Thought, 1830–1930.* And for a larger understanding of the creation of adolescence as a social construct, I am indebted to *The Rise and Fall of the American Teenager,* by Thomas Hine, among others.

One of the experiences that inspired me to write this book were my years teaching high school in the 1980s and 1990s, when my school was involved in attempting to redress what was then being called the "girls crisis," which suggested that the cause of the emotional withdrawal of girls during adolescence was the presence of boys in the classroom, and the ways in which teachers unintentionally privileged them. So I reread several of the books I studied in those years, among them *Failing at Fairness: How Our Schools Cheat Girls,* by Myra and David Sadker, as well as *Making Connections: The Relational Worlds of Adolescent Girls at Emma Willard School,* edited by Carol Gilligan, Nona P. Lyons, and Trudy J. Hammer, and *Reviving Ophelia: Saving the Selves of Adolescent Girls,* by Mary Pipher. In addition I reread Christina Hoff Sommers's *War Against Boys: How Misguided Feminism Is Harming Our Young Men,* which presents a compelling and countervailing argument to the one I had studied as a young teacher.

For readers interested in learning more about the subjects covered in *Girl Land,* I include here a short list of suggested reading:

Chapter Two: Dating

Allen, Frederick Lewis. *The Big Change: America Transforms Itself, 1900–1950.* Transaction, 1993.

Bailey, Beth L. *From Front Porch to Back Seat: Courtship in*

Twentieth-Century America. Johns Hopkins University Press, 1988.

Blanchard, Phyllis. *The Adolescent Girl: A Study from the Psychoanalytic Viewpoint*. Moffat, Yard, 1920.

Cameron, W. Bruce. *8 Simple Rules for Dating My Teenage Daughter*. Workman, 2001.

Craddock, Ida. "The Wedding Night," *Sexual Outlaw, Erotic Mystic: The Essential Ida Craddock*. Weiser, 2010.

DeLuzio, Crista. *Female Adolescence in American Scientific Thought, 1830–1930*. Johns Hopkins University Press, 2007.

Duvall, Evelyn Millis. *Love and the Facts of Life*. Association, 1963.

Gay, Peter. *Education of the Senses: The Bourgeois Experience, Victoria to Freud*. Oxford University Press, 1984.

Hall, G. Stanley. *Adolescence: Its Psychology and Its Relations to Physiology, Anthropology, Sociology, Sex, Crime, Religion, and Education*. Appleton, 1904.

Haupt, Enid A. *The Seventeen Book of Etiquette and Entertaining*. David McKay, 1963.

Morris, Lloyd. *Incredible New York: High Life and Low Life from 1850 to 1950*. Syracuse University Press, 1996.

Page, Ellen Welles. "A Flapper's Appeal to Parents," *Outlook,* December 6, 1922.

Sann, Paul. *The Lawless Decade: A Pictorial History of the Great American Transition, from the World War I Armistice and Prohibition to Repeal and the New Deal*. Outlet, 1957.

Smith, Betty. *Joy in the Morning*. Harper and Row, 1963.

Stone, Drs. Hannah and Abraham. *A Marriage Manual: A*

Practical Guidebook to Sex and Marriage. Simon and Schuster, 1939.

Chapter Three: Menstruation

Angier, Natalie. *Woman: An Intimate Geography.* Anchor, 1999.

Blume, Judy. *Are You There God? It's Me, Margaret.* Bantam Doubleday Dell, 1970.

Clarke, Edward H. *Sex in Education.* Wildside, 2007 (first edition, 1873).

Delaney, Janice, Mary Jane Lupton, and Emily Toth. *The Curse: A Cultural History of Menstruation.* University of Illinois Press, 1976.

Fessler, Ann. *The Girls Who Went Away: The Hidden History of Women Who Surrendered Children for Adoption in the Decades Before* Roe v. Wade. Penguin, 2006.

Freeman, Susan K. *Sex Goes to School.* University of Illinois Press, 2008.

Freidenfelds, Lara. *The Modern Period: Menstruation in Twentieth-Century America.* Johns Hopkins University Press, 2009.

Kermode, Mark. *The Exorcist.* British Film Institute, 1997.

Lee, Janet, and Jennifer Sasser-Coen. *Blood Stories: Menarche and the Politics of the Female Body in Contemporary U.S. Society.* Routledge, 1996.

Nalebuff, Rachel Kauder. *My Little Red Book.* Twelve, 2009.

Chapter Four: Diaries

American Girl. *A Smart Girl's Guide to Sticky Situations.* Turtleback, 2002.

Baskin, Julia, Lindsey Newman, Sophie Pollitt-Cohen, and Courtney Toombs. *The Notebook Girls: Four Friends. One Diary. Real Life.* Warner Books, 2006.

Brown, Sarah, ed. *Cringe: Teenage Diaries, Journals, Notes, Letters, Poems, and Abandoned Rock Operas.* Crown, 2008.

Brumberg, Joan Jacobs. *The Body Project: An Intimate History of American Girls.* Vintage, 1998.

Frank, Anne. *The Diary of a Young Girl, Definitive Edition.* Anchor Books, 1991.

Nin, Anaïs. *The Diary of Anaïs Nin.* Vol. 1, edited and with an introduction by Gunther Stuhlmann. Harcourt, 1966.

Novick, Peter. *The Holocaust in American Life.* Mariner, 2000.

Prose, Francine. *Anne Frank: The Book, The Life, The Afterlife.* Harper Collins, 2009.

Smith, Betty. *A Tree Grows in Brooklyn.* Harper and Brothers, 1943.

Wisenberg, S. L. *Holocaust Girls: History, Memory and Other Obsessions.* University of Nebraska Press, 2002.

Chapter Five: Sexual Initiation

Anonymous. *Go Ask Alice.* Simon and Schuster, 1971.

Bellah, Melanie. *Tammy: A Biography of a Young Girl.* Aten Press, 1999.

Blume, Judy. *Forever.* Simon and Schuster, 1975.

Cain, Chelsea, ed. *Wild Child: Girlhoods in the Counterculture.* Seal Press, 1999.

Calderone, Mary. "Sex Questions That Bother Boys," *Seventeen,* July 1969.

Gordon, Ernest. "The Feminine Art of Self-Defense." *Seventeen,* February 1969.

Graebner, William. *Patty's Got a Gun: Patricia Hearst in 1970s America.* University of Chicago Press, 2008.

Hearst, Patricia Campbell. *Every Secret Thing.* Doubleday, 1981.

Lemke-Santangelo, Gretchen. *Daughters of Aquarius: Women of the Sixties Counterculture.* University Press of Kansas, 2009.

Miles, Barry. *Hippie.* Sterling, 2003.

"Please Postpone the Wedding," *Seventeen,* September 1969.

Rynne, Tom. "If You're Thinking about Running Away from Home," *Seventeen,* February 1969.

Spock, Benjamin. *The Common Sense Book of Baby and Child Care.* Duell, Sloan and Pearce, 1946.

Talese, Gay. *Thy Neighbor's Wife.* Doubleday, 1980.

Chapter Six: Proms

Abell, Marietta, and Agnes J. Anderson. *The Junior-Senior*

Prom: Complete Practical Suggestions for Staging the Junior-Senior Prom. Northwestern Press, 1938.

Cohen, Robert, ed. *Dear Mrs. Roosevelt: Letters from Children of the Great Depression.* University of North Carolina Press, 2002.

Egan, Timothy. *The Worst Hard Time: The Untold Story of Those Who Survived the Great American Dust Bowl.* Houghton Mifflin, 2006.

Hine, Thomas, *The Rise and Fall of the American Teenager.* Avon, 1999.

Hobsbawm, Eric, and Terence Ranger, eds. *The Invention of Tradition.* Cambridge University Press, 1983.

Hulbert, Ann. "Take Back the Prom," Slate, November 3, 2005.

Inness, Sherrie A., ed. *Delinquents and Debutantes: Twentieth-Century American Girls' Cultures.* New York University Press, 1988.

Marling, Karal Ann. *Debutante: Rites and Regalia of American Debdom.* University of Kansas, 2004.

Schrum, Kelly. *Some Wore Bobby Sox: The Emergence of Teenage Girls' Culture, 1920–1945.* Palgrave Macmillan, 2004.

Chapter Seven: Moral Panics

I am indebted to Stanley Cohen's book *Folk Devils and Moral Panics* (MacGibbon and Kee, 1972) for its explanation of moral panic theory, which I used to understand the difference between the hysterical stories about group oral-sex parties (so prevalent in the first decade of this century) and the legitimate changes in teenagers' attitudes and practices regarding the act.

I also consulted the following books, articles, and documentaries: "The Sex Lives of Your Children" by Lucinda Franks in the February 2000 *Talk, In a Different Voice* by Carol Gilligan, *The Sensuous Woman* by J., "The Lost Children of Rockdale County" on *Frontline* in 1999, *Rainbow Party* by Paul Ruditis, and "They Say 'It's Not Sex,'" by Susan Weidman in the Winter 2003 issue of *Lilith*.

It is difficult to get exact numbers on teenagers and oral sex, and the subject is highly politicized because the trend is often presented as proof of the unintended and unpleasant consequences of abstinence-only sex-ed programs. There are, however, many studies to confirm the change in attitude and behavior:

- In September 2005, the National Center for Health Statistics investigated the topic of teenage oral sex more extensively than any previous study had and reported that a quarter of girls aged fifteen, and more than half aged seventeen, had engaged in it.
- Planned Parenthood's Info for Teens site reports that each month it receives hundreds of questions from teenagers about oral sex and that it concurs with the statistics of the NCHS study.
- A 2005 study of more than six hundred California

teenagers published in *The Journal of Pediatrics* found that a large number of these teenagers believed that oral sex was not "real sex," a finding consistent with a 1999 study of students at U.S. universities published in *The Journal of the American Medical Association.*

Three newspaper articles, two published in the *New York Times* and one in the *Washington Post* are often credited with being the first to bring attention to a possible, widespread change in teen behavior. They are:

Lewin, Tamar. "Teenagers Alter Sexual Practices, Thinking Risks Will Be Avoided," *New York Times,* April 5, 1997.

Stepp, Laura Sessions. "Parents Are Alarmed by an Unsettling New Fad in Middle Schools: Oral Sex," *Washington Post,* July 8, 1999.

Jarrell, Anne. "The Face of Teenage Sex Grows Younger," *New York Times,* April 2, 2000.

Acknowledgments

I've said it before and I'll say it again: I could not do this without Ben Schwarz. He is the best friend a writer could have: coming up with ideas, reading page after page, editing, coaxing, encouraging. I am so grateful to my dear friend Ben for all he did on this book and all he has done for my career as a writer—I wouldn't have one without him.

I'm in debt to the great people at Little, Brown, from Reagan Arthur, who has been a champion of my work from the very beginning, to Michael Pietsch, who has made such a fine home for me there. Jayne Yaffe Kemp did a wonderful job tightening and strengthening the manuscript, and I am grateful to her for her careful and insightful work. Jennifer

Rudolph Walsh has been fiercely supportive of this book for such a long time, even taking an early draft of it on vacation with her to the Yucatán Peninsula. I am really grateful to her for all she has done for me, and I have not said that enough. So I say it now: Jennifer, thank you.

I love *The Atlantic*. I've written for many places, and there's nowhere like it. First of all, Ben is there—but I'd love the *Penny Saver* if Ben were there. I've worked out many of the ideas in this book in the magazine's pages, and I'm so grateful to the late Mike Kelly, and to James Bennet, for all they have done for me. And, of course, I am eternally thankful to our godfather, David Bradley. I am more grateful to him than he will ever know.

My father told me I have a genius for friendship, and he was right. Here are some of the first-rate people that the genius has surrounded herself with: Lisan Cooper, Katherine Holmes-Chuba, Roberta Montgomery, Francie Norris, Tina Schwarz, Peggy Smith, and Sarah Timberman—you are the best friends anyone, anywhere, could ever have.

I have to give a second thank-you to Tina Schwarz: the best writer I know, and the best reader I will ever know. She read so many pages and improved so many sentences and cheered me through so many funks that I can only say thank you, Tina.

I am grateful to Chris "Sidebar" Cahill for his many insights into my subject, and for all the help he gave me while writing.

One day when I was writing this book, Ed Redlich dropped

by the house. I had just taped one hundred pages of manuscript on the hallway and living room floors and was pacing up and down, trying to get a look at them. He said, "Caitlin, are you losing your mind?" Yes, I was. So he and his wife, Sarah Timberman, gave me an extraordinary gift. The Glass House is now Los Angeles's premier book-finishing (and television-pilot writing/breakout dance session/wine tasting) location! You have to be losing your mind to get invited, but after that it's all gravy. On the losing-your-mind front: thanks to Anne Coscarelli for getting me on track and across the finish line! And thank you to Tania Breucop for amazing help in so many ways—it is deeply appreciated.

As ever, thanks to my family: to Rob, Patrick, and Conor; to my wonderful big sister, Ellen, and to the ones who have gone before us: Thomas and Jean Flanagan. Much missed, ever remembered.

Finally, to my muse and inspiration, Miss Julia Cooper, whose beautiful photograph (taken by her father, the brilliant photographer Andrew Cooper) graces the cover of this volume: thank you.

About the Author

Caitlin Flanagan is a former high school teacher who became a writer; she has been on staff at *The Atlantic, The New Yorker,* and the *Wall Street Journal*. A winner of the National Magazine Award, she has also written for *Time, O, The Oprah Magazine,* the *New York Times,* and the *Los Angeles Times*. Her work has been widely anthologized in, among other publications, *The Best American Essays* and *The Best American Magazine Writing* series. Her abiding interest in teenage girls led her to combine her passions for teaching and writing in *Girl Land*. She lives in Los Angeles with her husband and two sons.

Reading Group Guide

Girl Land

by

Caitlin Flanagan

A conversation with
Caitlin Flanagan

Former high school teacher turned *Atlantic* contributing editor Caitlin Flanagan dissects the harrowing world of female adolescence in her second book, *Girl Land*.

Weaving her own recollections of adolescence with on-the-ground research and history, Flanagan's portrait of this transitional period in a girl's life is a fascinating study of how society itself has changed—and not always for the better.

Flanagan spoke with us about the pitfalls of modern feminism, what's bad about the Internet, and why your teenage daughter might be off sulking in her bedroom.

You're looking at milestones of female adolescence here. Were there any aspects of this period that have changed so drastically it surprised you?

Almost everything! Look at menstruation. I'm fifty, and it was maybe a few years before I was born that it was still considered dangerous. It's a bittersweet feeling, the closer you are to giving life, the closer you are to potentially leaving your own.

There's still a sense that it's a time of profound reckoning in the life of the girl. With boys, [puberty] comes with pleasure and sexuality. With girls, it's blood.

We try to rush girls through things, and I feel sad and conflicted about that. The only positive is that girls' reproductive health is not nearly as dangerous as it once was. But we've failed to give girls the quiet and space to figure out what that all means to them, like we once did.

Are there other things that haven't much changed at all?

What hasn't changed is the enduring desire of a girl to withdraw during this time, to withdraw into herself, into her room. Parents might be used to having a daughter who was such a chatterbox, their constant companion. It's during this period that she retreats, goes into her bedroom, and closes the door. That's very constant. There's an understanding that this is a profound and scary change for her in a way that it's not for a boy. For girls, this period really affects the way they live, ends part of their lives. It's really different for boys.

Do you think that things have changed for boys in a similar manner? That their rites of passage have transformed in such a striking way?

Life's gotten a lot easier for boys. Ironically, what's made it a lot easier for them was done in the name of misguided feminism.

You're a vehement critic of modern feminism. You've said that "it's shortchanged a generation of women." How so?

I didn't say that feminism shortchanged a generation! It's been one of the most revolutionary and liberating forces in all of modern life. But I do think that some of the attitudes regarding sexuality that are usually identified as "feminist" have been at best misguided. The big thing I see on college campuses is that a lot of girls—the brightest and most capable who fought for admission to top schools, earned it on their own merits, and have huge altruistic goals—are uncomfortable with a normal part of their lives. They're drinking to black out with the intention of hooking up, going out, and having extremely sexual encounters with boys they don't know, or hardly know, that they barely remember the next day.

When I've talked to young women about their experiences, they often say, "It's empowering, it's our right, we can be as free as the guys get to be." If having this kind of semi-anonymous sex is part of the freedom that these girls earned from previous generations, there's something wrong with that.

Pornography, for example. Women watch it too. But the images you see on the screen don't have anything remotely to do with the sexual response of women. Body parts are slammed together; the prerogative of the sexual desire is built around the male desire. How can that be anything that's part of feminism?

So how do parents address the challenges their daughters face?

I've suggested that there should be no Internet in the girl's bedroom. And somehow it's become the most controversial thing I've said! Whether it's a smartphone or a laptop, Internet in the girl's bedroom is a bad idea—although it's so ubiquitous that getting it out of there is a tall order.

It's not just the extreme images. A girl needs a break, to come home at the end of the school day and just tune out. School is a lot more complicated and dramatic for girls than it is for boys. Their social lives are much more complex. They need a break after that, to be accepted on their own terms. They need space where they don't have be pretty, don't have to have the guy or sit at the right lunch table, where they can put on their stupid old sweatpants and their retainer.

That smartphone, that Facebook, that Twitter, doesn't allow that—it's coming in all the time, and it's extremely anxiety provoking. It's hard enough for adults to tune out, but terrible for adolescent girls. Parents give them these things, they have the right to say when and where and how they're going to be used. They'll have to deal with the fight that comes along with that. But it's in their daughter's best interest to draw boundaries, to have a least one space outside of that.

A version of this interview by Karen Calabria originally ran on the *Kirkus Reviews* website on January 12, 2012.

Questions and topics for discussion

1. What were the big milestones of your own Girl Land? Which ones were most significant? Which ones caused you the most excitement or the most anxiety?

2. How do you think these milestones have changed over time?

3. What does the word *prom* mean to you? If you went to your prom, how do you remember it? What was its meaning in your life at the time? Did it feel important, significant, or like just another event? If you haven't yet gone to a prom, what are your thoughts about it? Do you think you will go? What do your friends think and feel about prom?

4. How do you think menstruation has changed in the lives of girls over the past fifty years? What does the event mean to girls today? What did it mean to the girls of your mother's generation? Do you think that any girls still fear getting their period? Did you fear it at all?

5. Did you ever keep a diary? Do you keep one now? Do you keep a kind of online journal, via Facebook or another social-networking site? What's the emotional difference between a secret diary and an online diary? And if you have kept a secret diary, what kind of topics do you reserve for it? What do you think is behind the impulse to keep a journal?

6. Do you think high school–aged boys are more or less respectful of girls when it comes to the subject of sexuality? Have the positive changes in girls' lives extended to the way boys treat them in romantic or sexual relationships?

7. Do you think girls need special protection from the common culture of today—the hard-core material available online, for example, and the way it is changing how people look at young girls? What kind of protection would be in girls' best interest? And if we protect girls in a way that we don't also protect boys, are we therefore limiting their quality and empowerment?

Suggestions for further reading

Mrs. Mike, by Benedict and Nancy Freedman, 1947
Continuously in print since its publication, *Mrs. Mike*—set in the wild and dangerous territory around Alberta, Canada, at the turn of the last century—combines adventure and romance, and it has delighted generations of girl readers.

The Bell Jar, by Sylvia Plath, 1963
Sylvia Plath's autobiographical novel about high intelligence, female ambition, and crippling depression.

Go Ask Alice, by Anonymous, 1971
Hailed by the *New York Times* at its publication as "a document of horrifying reality," *Go Ask Alice* reflects in equal parts the truth and the hysteria surrounding drug use by adolescent girls in the years immediately following the 1960s.

Stop That Girl, by Elizabeth McKenzie, 2005
Stop That Girl is a hilarious coming-of-age novel, told in a

series of short stories about a peerless heroine named Ann Ransom. Readers of all ages will love it.

The Modern Period: Menstruation in Twentieth-Century America, **by Lara Freidenfelds, 2009**
An excellent social history of American attitudes toward menstruation and of the feminine hygiene industry that served to both capitalize on and shape those attitudes.

My Little Red Book, **by Rachel Kauder Nalebuff, 2009**
An anthology of stories about first periods, *My Little Red Book* has become a classic among young girls awaiting the start of menstruation.

The Body Project: An Intimate History of American Girls, **by Joan Jacobs Brumberg, 1998**
A definitive and very readable book on girls' history by a renowned scholar in the field.

Some Wore Bobby Socks: The Emergence of Teenage Girls' Culture, 1920–1945, **by Kelly Schrum, 2004**
Schrum describes the development of a separate material and popular culture devoted specifically to teenage girls, with chapters on fashion, beauty, music, and the movies.

From Front Porch to Back Seat: Courtship in Twentieth-Century America, **by Beth L. Bailey, 1988**
An excellent, concise history of dating, from chaperoned

visits in the family parlor to the emergence of car culture.

The Girls Who Went Away: The Hidden History of Women Who Surrendered Children for Adoption in the Decades before **Roe v. Wade, by Ann Fessler, 2006**

A heartbreaking collection of interviews with women who were forced to surrender their babies as pregnant teenagers in the decades before legalized abortion in this country,

Also by Caitlin Flanagan

To Hell with All That: Loving and Loathing Our Inner Housewife

"Flanagan writes with intelligence, wit and brio. She's likable....What makes Flanagan's book original and vital is that she is a realist, willing to acknowledge the essential gray areas in too often polarized positions."
— *New York Times Book Review*

"One of the liveliest and most controversial essayists on the scene."
— *Dallas Morning News*

"Flanagan is an immensely appealing writer and social observer."
— *Wall Street Journal*

"A sparkling writer with an incisive wit....Flanagan's a contrarian and frequently brave."
— *Philadelphia Inquirer*

Back Bay Books • Available wherever paperbacks are sold